GET THE BALL ROLLING

A Step by Step Guide to Training for Treibball

Dianna Stearns, M.A. CPDT-KA, CDBC, CATT

Dogwise™ Publishing

Wenatchee, Washington U.S.A.

Get the Ball Rolling
A Step by Step Guide to Training for Treibball
Dianna Stearns, M.A. CPDT-KA, CDBC, CATT

Dogwise Publishing
A Division of Direct Book Service, Inc.
403 South Mission Street, Wenatchee, Washington 98801
1-509-663-9115, 1-800-776-2665
www.dogwisepublishing.com / info@dogwisepublishing.com

© 2013 Dianna Stearns
Cover illustration: Michael Curran, ClickerLogicInc.
Graphic design: Lindsay Peternell
Cover design: Brittney Kind

Library of Congress Cataloging-in-Publication Data
Stearns, Dianna, 1947-
  Get the ball rolling : a step by step guide to training for treibball / Dianna Stearns, M.A. CPDT-KA, CDBC, CATT.
    pages cm
  Includes bibliographical references and index.
  ISBN 978-1-61781-111-1
  1. Treibball (Dog sport) 2. Dogs--Training. I. Title.
  SF425.85.T74S74 2013
  636.7'0887--dc23
                          2012041506

ISBN: 978-1-61781-111-1

Printed in the U.S.A.

This book is dedicated to Skippy, Nimrodel, Barnaby, Shelley, Pepper, Holly, Henry and Zoe, who came before, and to Terry, Chance, Huerro and Fin who came after.

They have all taught me, their student, with infinite patience and unyielding devotion.

TABLE OF CONTENTS

ACKNOWLEDGMENTS

In development of anything new, the concerted efforts of many enthusiastic, caring and talented people have been needed and are greatly appreciated.

This curriculum would not exist without the efforts of Hilary Lane and Mary Manka, my co-founders of the American Treibball Association. My heartfelt thanks to you for the hours of time and attention you have given to this project.

My thanks also go out to our outstanding students/trainers and their dogs, who have served as guinea pigs, patient class participants and ultimately our best models. They have contributed practical ideas and valuable insights in developing the curriculums. My grateful thanks go out to Will and Eloise, Gina and Sakara, Mary and Winston, Timmie and Izzie, Kim and Kita, Sally and Ike, Mary and Jack and to my own patient dogs, the perfect Chance and newbie Fin.

Kudos must be given to our official photographer, Fred Stearns, of Stearns Photography. Shooting dogs in motion is always a challenge. Fred has met that challenge with exceeding skill, grace and good humor. Thanks also to his daughter, talented graphic designer, Alice Stearns, for her diagrams, which will give students an overhead view of the playing field for more exact ball and handler placement.

Finally, my thanks go out to you who are reading this. If you are open to learning something new and committed to working and playing with your dog in a non-violent manner that strengthens the communication and loving bond between you, you are making the world a better place.

INTRODUCTION

Welcome to the new, all-positive sport of Treibball, a team dog activity derived from herding trials that uses exercise balls rather than sheep and a soccer goal rather than a pen. Teaching your dog to "herd" the balls into the goal is great fun for both you and your dog, and he does not need to be member of the Herding group to succeed. Beyond the fun involved, what makes Treibball so great is that it builds your dog's attention to you, his impulse control and off-leash reliability. And most importantly, it strengthens the level of communication between the two of you. Treibball is a thinking game; it is a conversation between you and your dog, with smooth teamwork as the real goal.

Treibball is fun, but is complex (at first!). Take your time and be patient with your dog and yourself. It's a new skill for both of you! While the competitions are timed, practicing the skills needed to play should be done slowly. You may already be using some of the basic obedience cues used in Treibball, while some, the herding cues, may be new to you. As with any skill, there's a learning curve at the beginning, which levels off, then moves along quickly as you practice. Move forward only as your dog's level of enthusiasm and accomplishment increases. Make sure he is solid at each stage before pressing him to do more. If, at any time, you and your dog are *not having fun* working together, stop. Go back to the point at which you were having fun and practice again before moving on. After your dog makes the connection between your verbal cues and making the ball move in a specific direction toward you to get a reward, you'll really begin to have fun with the game. From that point on, it's just a matter of teamwork, coordination and timing to play against the clock.

The Treibball training curriculum I teach is a progressive, clicker-based program. The lessons start with relatively simple foundation behaviors and verbal cues that you and your dog may already know. The advanced lessons involve more complex challenges including directing your dog at a distance, specific ball control skills, precise body-positioning and the fine-tuning necessary to sharpen both your skills for playing this competitive game. The exercises are broken down into individual steps so that if you need more time to work on any individual component, you and your dog can progress at a speed that works for you.

I recommend a training method known as **shaping**, in which the trainer moves or lures the dog into a specific position she wishes to reinforce, then **marks** the correct response with a clicker and offers a reward, and then adds or teaches the verbal cue for that behavior. This technique is used to "get" or "capture" a behavior, then mark and reward each individual step (or each correct attempt) in small increments. The goal is then to link each step into a completed behavior.

In many of these introductory exercises, "free shaping" can be used to great advantage in order to create a relationship between the dog and the ball and to position the dog correctly behind it. Free shaping is a technique in which the handler waits for the dog to perform a desired action on his own before reinforcing him for that action. In other exercises, a combination of shaping and "luring" can be used to encourage the dog to make the correct choice and offer the desired behavior. Whether you free shape or lure a behavior, I recommend that the handler reinforce the behavior several times with a click and reward before adding a verbal cue as this technique has been shown to build more reliable behaviors over the long run.

This book is organized into five parts as follows:

1. The **Treibball Overview** presents information on the development of the sport in Europe and a summary of the rules of the sport as it is currently played in the United States.

2. **Training Basics** provides an overview of the modern positive training method I recommend.

3. The **Introductory Treibball** section teaches you the basic cues, body positioning, movements and beginning ball-handling skills that lay a foundation for playing the game.

4. The **Intermediate Level Treibball** section is the point in your training in which the distance between you and your dog increases, as does the dog's physical control, timing and skill in moving multiple balls to you at the goal.

5. The **Advanced Level Treibball** section provides enhancements to the game including physical and mental challenges to you and your dog's problem solving skills.

In this book, your dog is referred to in the masculine simply for ease of reference. No inference should be made as to the suitability of one sex over another. It is simply too cumbersome to reframe every sentence with "he/she" or "him/her." Female dogs excel at Treibball as well as males and every dog can have equal fun playing the game.

All verbal instructions or cues are shown in quotation marks, as in **"Come Bye!"** The behavior itself is shown in bold within the context of the exercise. For example, send your dog to **Come Bye!** Key training and behavior terms are bolded upon first use and included in the glossary. Italics are used for emphasis.

The directions given refer to the handler's viewpoint of the field, from your position at the goal. When the exercise says move the dog "right," it always means to move him to *your* right, or clockwise. When the exercise says to move the dog "left," it always means to move him to *your* left, or counterclockwise.

1

What Is Treibball? An Overview

Treibball (pronounced Try-ball) is a new competitive dog sport for dogs of all ages and sizes. It is great fun for *any* energetic dog who can learn to work well off-leash, loves to play chase games, loves to herd or who just needs a job! Fun and communication between the human and canine partners is the true essence of this game. Treibball is a positive, fun sport that builds a great working relationship between owner and dog.

Treibball was developed in Germany about ten years ago by Dutch dog trainer Jan Nijboer (www.Natural-Dogmanship.com). He noticed the dogs he trained often still had excess energy after their herding lessons were over. Instead of playing with their training dummies, they made up their own herding game by pushing objects around the field, and seemed to enjoy the act of pushing as much as the actual herding. Nijboer had watched a television show that featured two Boxer dogs playing soccer in which they tried to push a ball into a goal. He wondered if herding dogs would do the same thing, using large fitness balls instead of sheep. He visualized them essentially playing soccer, moving balls toward a goal under the control of a handler similar to how sheep are herded into pens by herding dogs. Finding that his dogs could be trained to do this, he incorporated balls of different sizes into his herding practice and developed the game for his training clients. The game caught on in Germany and spread to Holland and Scandinavia. The first international Treibball competition was held in Sweden in 2007. A Treibball video, *"Hund mit 8 Ballen,"* appeared on the internet in late 2009 and quickly went viral. The game is continuing to evolve in Europe with variations in play, competition and class practice.

As an American trainer I asked, "Why should European dogs have all the fun?" Our dogs have excess energy too and don't always have an outlet for it. Our modern, sedentary lifestyles, for the most part, are not healthy for us or our pets. Most dog breeds evolved over time or were genetically bred to do a job. Dogs need mental stimulation and physical activity to lead full lives, and the majority of American dogs simply don't get it. Training and competing in Treibball is low cost and low impact on you (the handler) *and* your dog. Playing Treibball will be a good fit for many dogs and handlers!

Playing Treibball

Treibball can be thought of as a combination of a herding trial and a canine soccer match. The object of the game is for the dog to drive eight fitness balls, which are placed in the middle of a field, into a soccer-style goal within a ten-minute time period. The dog moves the balls under the direction of a handler who remains relatively stationary in the goal. The competition is judged with a dog's score dependent on how quickly he drives the balls into the goal and whether or not certain defined errors on the part of the dog or handler are committed.

The game can be played on any level surface, such as grass, rubber matting, asphalt or sand. The field can be of varied sizes, but typically is 75 feet long and 50 feet wide. To begin, the eight fitness-type balls are arranged in a triangle, midfield from the goal, with the point of the triangle facing away from the goal (like in billiards). The balls can be of differing sizes or all the same size, however they should be appropriate to the size of the dog. If you visualize the playing field as the face of a circular clock, the handler's position is the center of the goal at 6 o'clock. He/she can move within a four foot area of the goal—to the left, right or center from the 6 o'clock position, but cannot enter further into the field. The balls are aligned in the center of the field, half way between the 6 and the 12 o'clock positions. The dog begins at the middle-left of the field, at the 10 o'clock position. At the Timekeeper's signal, the handler sends the dog to his right, past the field of balls to the 12 o'clock position. The handler must communicate effectively with verbal commands, hand signals or whistles to cue the dog which direction to move and which ball to bring in. The handler may use a staff to help guide the balls into the goal when the dog brings them close, but cannot step into the playing field. The game stops when ten minutes have elapsed or when all eight balls are in the goal. Then the dog lies down in front of the goal, like penning sheep!

Treibball rules, the short version (see Appendix for a complete set of rules)

As game inventor Jan Nijboer says, Treibball is meant to be a sport played "in cooperation with the dog handler. The way you communicate with your dog is essential, not how many goals you achieve!" In keeping with Mr. Nijboer's original intent, improving the communications skills that enhance the dog-human bond are the real goals of the American Treibball Association (ATA). Treibball is supposed to be fun—for you *and* for your dog.

In Treibball, one dog and one handler compete against the clock per round of play. Total run time consists of ten minutes. The game begins when the handler signals the Timekeeper he is ready. The run time begins when the Timekeeper then signals the handler to send the dog from the start position midfield to move behind the eight balls that are set out in the form of a triangle (like pool/billiards). The dog is asked to drive each ball into the goal. The handler stands and moves within the goal area, changing his position left, right and center but is not allowed to enter further into the field. The handler guides the dog by voice or hand signal and both handler and dog are expected to work together as a team. If all eight balls are driven into the goal within ten minutes, the dog is directed to lie down at the goal line and the run is over. If the dog is still attempting to drive balls into the goal when there are ten minutes on the clock, time is called and the run is over.

A match should be played on a level, non-slip surface (sand, grass, artificial turf, asphalt) that provides safety for the dogs and handlers. The field of play is 75 feet long by 50 feet wide for dogs over 17.1 inches in height. Smaller dogs, 17 inches and under, play on a field 40 feet long by 50 feet wide. All dogs compete in size and age appropriate categories.

The eight balls are placed mid-field in a triangle, with the point/peak ball farthest from the goal. The balls can be of differing sizes or all the same size. An appropriate sized ball is one where the mid-point of the ball should be no higher than the level of the dog's nose. An assortment of ball sizes makes it more fun!

For Standard competition:
All dogs over 17.1 inches (measured at the shoulder)

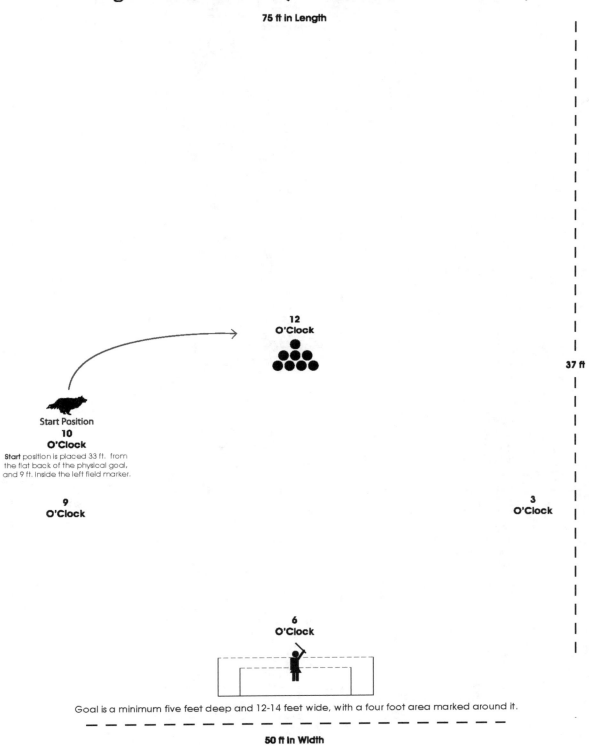

75 ft in Length

12
O'Clock

37 ft

Start Position
10
O'Clock

Start position is placed 33 ft. from
the flat back of the physical goal,
and 9 ft. inside the left field marker.

9
O'Clock

3
O'Clock

6
O'Clock

Goal is a minimum five feet deep and 12-14 feet wide, with a four foot area marked around it.

50 ft in Width

For Teacup competition:
All small dogs under 17 inches (measured at the shoulder)

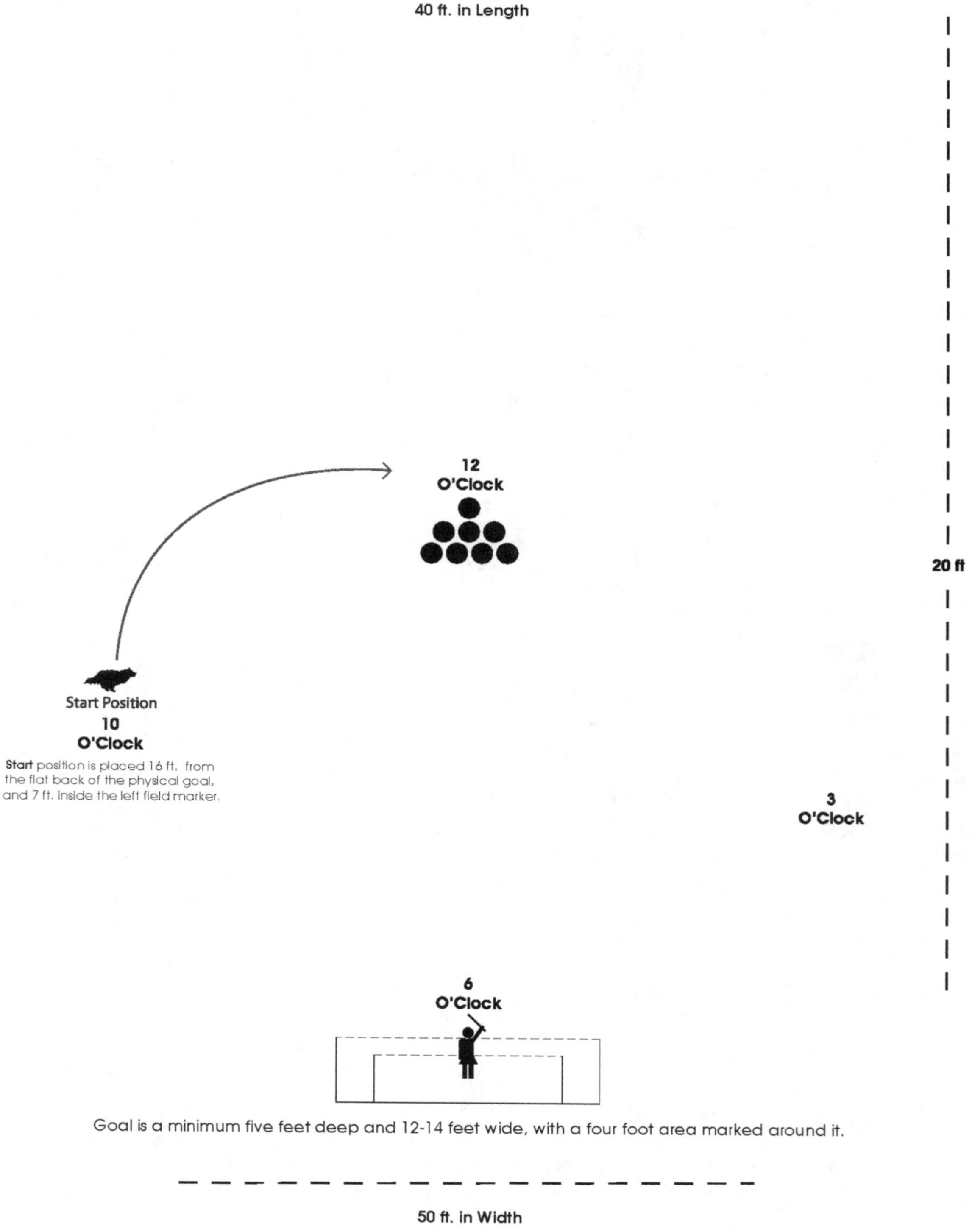

40 ft. in Length

12 O'Clock

Start Position 10 O'Clock

Start position is placed 16 ft. from the flat back of the physical goal, and 7 ft. inside the left field marker.

20 ft

3 O'Clock

6 O'Clock

Goal is a minimum five feet deep and 12-14 feet wide, with a four foot area marked around it.

50 ft. in Width

Goals should be a minimum of four to five feet deep by twelve to fourteen feet long. A regulation sized soccer goal may be used. Chalk or tape may be used to define the entire goal area.

The dog's handler is allowed to move within a four foot area, left right or center of the physical goal, but is not allowed to move into the field of play.

If the dog drives all the balls into the goal within the allotted ten minute time period, his run is scored based on how many seconds faster than the ten minutes he took to complete his run. For example, the dog earns three bonus points if he drives the ball forward with only one signal from the handler. Based on the time of his run and accumulated bonus/demerit points, the dog with the lowest time wins.

Bonus and demerit points are important elements of the score, as each point amounts to fifteen seconds being added or subtracted to the dog's time. Demerits are charged for things like the handler putting pressure on the dog by voice or gesture, the dog starting at the wrong side of the triangle or the handler entering the field of play beyond four feet from the goal.

A team can be disqualified if the dog bites the balls or if the handler reprimands or punishes the dog physically.

The judges are given some discretion over the rules, bonuses and demerits as well as disqualifications if they are acting in the best interest of the dog.

The complete set of ATA rules and recommendations located at the back of this book are current as of publication date of this book. The rules are subject to change yearly by the full voting membership of the Association, and the latest version will always be posted on the Association's website at www.americantreibballassociation.org for free public download. See the section below for more information on the ATA.

Please note that Treibball as an organized sport is still in its infancy in the United States. While the basics of the game are pretty well established, you might find that the rules you encounter at an independent, non-sanctioned match or competition might vary from the ATA rules. The sport is continuing to evolve as it grows.

Is Treibball the right sport for you and your dog?

To be successful in Treibball, your dog should have some off-leash reliability to start. It is clear that achieving off-leash reliability will be more difficult with some breeds or individual dogs than with others. It is no surprise that Treibball was developed with Herding dogs in mind. What makes Treibball challenging is that the dog is working off-leash at a distance from the handler during the competition, and the only means by which the handler can direct the dog is through verbal cues, whistles or hand signals—no physical manipulation of the dog is allowed. The better communication between the dog and handler, the more fluid the movement and the faster the times!

Many of the skills required in Treibball are relatively easy to teach and your dog may already know them. Any dog that can "target" an object or your hand and knows how to **Sit**, **Stand**, lie **Down** and **Watch** already knows the basic obedience components used in Treibball. It is also easy to get started in Treibball; with a just few balls from the exercise equipment section of your local retailer, a clicker and some treats, you can begin training.

Whether or not the training program is easy for you and your dog to learn, Treibball brings many additional benefits. Since Treibball is a positive sport with no physical or verbal corrections allowed, it is an excellent vehicle for encouraging reward-based training and creative play between owners and their dogs. My clients tell me that learning and playing Treibball has had many benefits, most notably improvements in the dog's ability to focus on taking direction and improving the dog's off-leash reliability. As I saw my clients responding to Treibball as a problem-solving game, my colleagues and I became determined to take the sport to the next level by forming an organization to improve and promote the sport.

The American Treibball Association

The American Treibball Association (ATA), a member-centered, non-profit organization, was established in August of 2010 to promote and develop the game of Treibball in the United State. The goals of the ATA are to use the sport of Treibball to: (1) be a positive teaching tool; (2) provide a calm, low-impact game for dog owners to play; (3) offer a positive reinforcement sport for progressive dog trainers to teach; and (4) create a competitive challenge for dog-sports enthusiasts to enhance their relationships with their dogs.

The ATA is also focused on publicizing and promoting the sport of Treibball, establishing official rules and standards for play in the United States, hosting regional and national competitions and awarding titles in the sport. The ATA is currently the only member-centered training and competition organization for dog owners and trainers in the United States devoted to the sport.

The ATA also certifies American Treibball Trainers for teaching the training curriculum and judging competitions. Dog owners, professional trainers and training facilities are encouraged to join the Association to build the sport in this country. Our vision is that Treibball will continue to grow and evolve in the United States, both as a competitive sport and as a vehicle for positive reinforcement training.

Interested readers can get additional information and watch a wide assortment of videos by visiting the Association's website, www.americantreibballassociation.org, the ATA's Facebook page, www.facebook.com/americantreibball or the YouTube channel www.youtube.com/user/AmericanTreibball.

2

Training Basics for Treibball

This section presents an overview of the training method I believe will lead you to the most success in Treibball. I am a proponent of clicker training; I believe in the total avoidance of any forceful methods as well as those that involve excessive verbal or any physical corrections. Since so many of the behaviors your dog needs to learn are done at such a distance from you, forceful methods and corrections are not only ineffective, but are in fact counterproductive in creating a loving bond with your dog and training a fun activity.

Clicker training is generally described as a method of developing desired behaviors using a simple sound as an indicator that the dog has done something right. A click, whistle or any other distinctive sound is used to **mark** the behavior you want to reinforce. The clicker is particularly useful in training behaviors at a distance since the sound is clean, and unlike the human voice, carries crisply indoors and out. Clicker training is used in this curriculum because it is a great technique to: (1) help build **fluency** at a distance; (2) mark the desired behavior as it happens; and (3) gain competency in the shortest time. The presence or absence of the click speaks volumes since a click is always followed by some type of reward. Clickers can be purchased at any major pet retailer, most independent pet stores or online.

If you've never used a clicker before when training your dog, you may ask *"Why do I need something else to handle while training, when I already have a leash and treats to deliver? Why should I use a clicker when I can always use my voice to give my dog a verbal marker?"* The click is a neutral sound and takes the place of a slower, spoken response. Unlike a clicker, your tone of voice is variable. It changes, depending on the time of day, or whether you're tired, angry, frustrated or happy. Those changes make it virtually impossible to deliver a verbal marker like *"Good Boy"* or *"Yes!"* to your dog in the same tone of voice each time. Your verbal marker may, at different times, have subtle, different meanings. Dogs are constantly attuned to your tone of voice and body language when interpreting your directions, which are not always consistent. Using a clicker to train your dog produces behaviors of cleaner precision, because your dog understands exactly what he needs to do to be rewarded. Your training then becomes a natural dialogue; he looks to you for direction (what you're asking for) and then gets an immediate confirmation that he gave you the right response. While verbal praise and physical interaction can still be used, it is the reward or reinforcement your dog is working for. Praise and petting should come after his work is done.

It's important to remember that the clicker is a **secondary reinforcer** or a bridge. It is used to mark the desired behavior with precision to inform the dog that the **primary reinforcer**—his treat, toy or other reward—is coming immediately. The click is *not* used to get the dog's attention. The click is an unambiguous message, and is purely informational. It is *not praise*.

You can use a clicker to shape and reinforce behaviors whether they are lured or captured. Many trainers "lure" their dogs into sitting, lying down or hand targeting with food. As the dog completes the desired behavior he is clicked and treated. Other behaviors are trained more efficiently using capturing. Examples could be scratching, yawning or performing a play bow. Whether you lure or capture the behavior you want to train, it is (1) having the dog repeat the behavior, and (2) consistently reinforcing it, that leads to learning. Once the dog is doing the behavior you want consistently, you can begin to use a verbal **cue** to name the behavior and begin to **fade** (reduce the frequency of) clicking and rewarding. At any time, you may use a verbal cue your dog knows such as "Wait" or the "Watch me" cue, before adding an additional cue.

Over time, the knowledge the dog gains from the sound of a clicker is immediate and self-reinforcing. The click becomes as powerful as the reward and the dog begins to work for the sound. As your dog becomes more proficient at the game and the individual behaviors are linked into fluid movements, you will fade the use of the clicker completely and substitute suitable verbal markers and praise to keep him motivated. You will be moving your dog from continuous marking and reinforcing to verbal feedback and praise, with his physical reward occurring only on the full completion of each task.

Training tips and guidelines

A good clicker trainer must be a keen observer of her dog. You know him best, so it should not be difficult. If you're going to reward him for his correct responses, you need to be aware of exactly what he is doing while you're training him in order to deliver the click on time and reward him immediately. This becomes even *more* important should you decide *not* to use a clicker and substitute only verbal cues instead. You'll need good timing and you have to be generous, not stingy, with your treats and loving attention.

Training any new behavior takes patience and strong powers of observation on *your* part. It takes skill to mark and reward the exact behavior or position you want your dog to learn. Applied animal behaviorists and veterinary behaviorists tell us that any behavior that is marked and rewarded within three to five seconds of occurring makes that behavior most likely to be repeated. In this curriculum, strive for three to five seconds as the optimum timing for the marking of the behavior and the delivery of the dog's reward. Don't worry if your coordination or timing is not perfect at first; your dog will still learn and respond.

Good trainers use *lots* of reinforcement! There's an old trainer's saying that goes "The most generous trainers have the best trained dogs." You will not spoil your dog by using treats. Once the behavior is reliably on cue, you will be able to fade some rewards entirely and vary the rate of others. Good trainers use many different kinds of reinforcements. Anything your dog enjoys can be used to reinforce the behavior you want; use his favorite toys, tummy rubs, lots of praise or an extra game of tug. Do some experimenting and then work his favorite rewards into your training sessions.

As you begin to teach any new behavior, each successful step should be clicked and rewarded immediately. Keep your rate of reinforcement *very high*. For example, click and reward for five to ten successful repetitions. Once your dog is successful consistently at any given step, you can add a verbal cue and begin to reward on a more intermittent basis (for example, click and treat half the time the dog gets it right).

When teaching a multi-step behavior, wait until your dog is successful 80% of the time at any given step (i.e., he performed correctly four out of five times) before moving on to the next step. This makes it easier to link (chain) each step of more complex behaviors.

The concept of **raising criteria** is one trainers use when beginning to ask a dog to perform more difficult behaviors. If you don't raise your criteria gradually, your dog may get frustrated. When asking for a more difficult behavior, increase your rate of reinforcement again until he is successful once again at the 80% level. Each time the task becomes harder, the dog will require more input and direction to accomplish it. Don't be in a hurry. Allow your dog to build competence though repetition and consistency at each stage of his training and you'll both have more success and fun. Once all the individual steps have been chained into a complex behavior, the behavior has been put on cue and the dog is responding in the appropriate fashion, raise your criteria again. Reward only the final step of a complex behavior when the dog has shown he can complete the entire exercise.

Any time your dog shows fear or unwillingness to complete a task, you may have gone too fast, raised your criteria too high, varied your rate of reward too much or applied too much pressure. If this happens, go back and break that same behavior down into smaller steps and raise your rate of reward. Mark and reward every incremental step to build your dog's confidence, and encourage him to have fun with you, which is the object of the game! *Relax, have fun and enjoy building a better working relationship with your dog!*

Since we know dogs are not verbal learners, adding the verbal cue for the behavior is less important than actually achieving the behavior. In most forms of positive reinforcement training, trainers strive for 80% reliability in the task before adding the verbal cue that describes that task. Since humans are verbal learners, I suggest using the verbal cues in this curriculum along with the accompanying movements for ease of understanding. If you wish to only use hand signals and body movements without verbal cues until you have 80% reliability, you are encouraged to do that.

Your home training sessions should range from ten to fifteen minutes at a time, at least once a day. If you want to train more, limit yourself to three to five sessions a day, maximum. Keep your training sessions light and fun so your dog doesn't get bored but wants to do more! Work two to three minutes on each task, and then give your dog a break. If your dog cannot accomplish the step you're working on, find something he *can* do and end your ten to fifteen minute session on a positive note. Mark and reward something simple (even if it's a **Sit** or **Down**) and then use a **release word** to let him know he is done working for a while. In Treibball, we use the herding term **"That'll Do!"** to release the dog from the required behavior, but you may use a term your dog already knows, such as **"Free," "Finish"** or **"All Done,"** if you prefer.

As you practice with your dog, I encourage you to work in the manner and at the pace that is most comfortable for you. In dog training, there is no "one-size-fits-all." Because each dog and trainer learns at his or her own pace, I suggest a minimum of five repetitions for most exercises. This will keep you moving as each exercise builds on the one that came before. If it takes you and your dog more or less repetition to achieve 80% reliability, let practice be your guide.

Remember that Treibball should be trained using a *positive reinforcement curriculum*. There is no jerking, no physical correction, punishment, verbal reprimanding, shouting or any intimidation of dogs allowed in Treibball. Be patient with your dog and yourself. It's a new skill for both of you!

Training Sessions 10-15 min at least 1x/day
3-5 x/day max

2-3 min. ea. task then break

3

Introductory Treibball Training

The Introductory section teaches the core behaviors that lay the foundation for playing Treibball. Some of you may have already taught your dog many of these basic obedience behaviors, using cues such as **Watch me, Down, Stand** or **Back/Back-up**. For others, these may cues be new to you, but will be usable in any kind of training you choose to do.

In addition, we'll be introducing some herding behaviors and cues not many are familiar with; such as **Come Bye** for moving the dog to your right, and **Away to Me** for moving the dog to your left. Learning these new cues could be a bit overwhelming a first, but don't be confused by any jargon. If there are equivalent cues your dog already knows and responds to, feel free to use them instead. Whatever terms and cues you use, be sure to use them consistently and work with your dog on these foundation behaviors before competing in a Treibball event.

The lessons and exercises included in this section are as follows:

- Lesson 1
  - Charging or loading the clicker
  - Watch me!
  - Hand targeting
  - Transferring the Touch cue to a target stick
  - Introducing That'll Do! for release

- Lesson 2
  - Dog orients his body to your right
  - Dog orients his body to your left

- Lesson 3
  - Dog lines up behind the ball
  - Dog touches his nose to the ball and nudges it forward
  - Introducing the verbal cue for moving right, Come Bye!, and left, Away to Me

- Lesson 4
  - Dog moves to your right on cue/using target stick (Come Bye!)
  - Dog moves to your left on cue/using target stick (Away to Me!)

- ○ Combine Away to Me! and Line-up with Touch
- ○ Combine Come Bye! and Line-up with Touch

- Lesson 5
  - ○ Dog remains in standing position
  - ○ Dog moves counterclockwise to stand behind ball
  - ○ Dog moves clockwise to stand behind ball
  - ○ Dog drives the ball toward goal

- Lesson 6
  - ○ Dog changes direction around the ball, left and right
  - ○ Dog moves right, drives ball and lies down at goal line
  - ○ Dog moves left, drives ball and lies down at goal line

- Lesson 7
  - ○ Dog backs up in straight line and stays
  - ○ Dog backs up and then approaches ball
  - ○ Combine Back with Come Bye!, Stand, Drive! and That'll Do

- Lesson 8
  - ○ Down and That'll Do
  - ○ Drive!, Down and That'll Do
  - ○ Stand, Drive!, Down and That'll Do
  - ○ Back, Stand, Drive!, Down and That'll Do
  - ○ Come Bye!, Stand, Back or Walk-on!, Drive!, Down and That'll Do
  - ○ Away to Me!, Stand, Back or Walk-on!, Drive!, Down and That'll Do

Lesson 1

All training begins with attention. In the first lesson, your dog will learn that looking at you and participating with you makes a click happen and that the click means good things happen for him. The more this happens, the more his attention span will increase. You will become the source of all good things—fun, treats and ultimately learning.

Exercise 1: Charging or loading the clicker

Goal: Teach your dog that the click means that a treat is coming!

This exercise can easily be done at home, when you're watching TV, cooking dinner or doing any household activity where your dog is in close proximity. By using the clicker to confirm his attention to you, you're teaching him that he does not have to give you his attention all the time, but when you ask for it, he should! The more this happens, the more his attention to you will increase.

Step 1: Say your dog's name when he is not looking at you. When he turns his head to look at you, click and toss a treat on the ground or offer him one with your hand.

Step 2: If you are already using a release word with your dog, use it to let him know you're finished for that time period. If you are not yet using a release word, introduce the herding cue **"That'll Do!"** as a release.

Practice five to ten minutes, several times a day. Say his name and click when he looks at you, then immediately reward and release him.

Exercise 2: Watch me! Part One

Chance practices Watch me!

Goal: Your dog gives you his complete attention (eye contact) upon request, then is released using **That'll Do!**

Step 1: Ask your dog to **Sit** in front of you. When he sits, take a treat and move it from the tip of his nose to up between your eyes.

Step 2: Say **"<Your dog's name>, Watch me!"** When your dog's eyes center on your face and make direct eye contact with you, click, then open your hand, and say **"Take it."** Allow him to take the treat.

Step 3: Say your release cue **"That'll Do!"** and take a few steps away from the dog.

Step 4: Repeat Step 2, but require your dog to hold his gaze for a count of three seconds. After each repetition, at the end of your count say **"That'll Do!"** to release your dog.

Practice five to ten minutes several times a day. Try rewarding varying durations of attention to you: five seconds, ten seconds, three seconds, twenty seconds, eight seconds and then building up to a solid fifteen to thirty seconds of eye contact, before rewarding and releasing your dog. At the end of each count (whatever count you're using), say **"That'll Do!"** to release your dog.

Exercise 2: Watch me! Part Two

Watch me! with larger hand signal and arm extended.

Goal: Your dog will give you his complete attention (eye contact) upon request with a larger, more visible hand signal and a food distraction at the side.

In this exercise, we're introducing a larger, more visible hand signal that can be seen from a greater distance.

Step 1: Ask your dog to **Sit** in front of you. When he sits, hold a treat between your thumb and forefinger in one hand out at arm's length. Move your other hand upright, with your index finger pointing up between your eyes or at the tip of your nose.

Step 2: Say **"<Your dog's name>, Watch me!"** When your dog's eyes come back to center on your face and he makes direct eye contact with you, click immediately. Open your hand flat, say **"Take it"** and allow your dog to take the treat.

Step 3: Now repeat and hold your dog's gaze for a count of five seconds. At the end of the count, click, then open your left hand and say **"Take it"** and allow your dog to take the treat.

Step 4: After your last repetition (whatever count you may be working on), say **"That'll Do!"** to release your dog.

Step 5: Once the behavior is on cue, and your dog has achieved 80% reliability, raise your criteria and mark and reward him for faster and faster responses. As he becomes more experienced at this, you will notice that his head remains in one position and only his eyes move. Once he becomes an expert at watching you, his eyes *never even leave your face!*

Practice five to ten minutes, several times a day, rewarding your dog for varying amounts of eye contact: five seconds, then ten, fifteen, twenty, twenty-five and finally thirty seconds of eye contact before rewarding and releasing him.

Exercise 3: Hand targeting

Fin moves and left and right touching the hand target on cue.

Goal: Your dog will touch his nose to your hand on cue.

Now we introduce the concept of **targeting**, giving you dog an object or a focus point to direct his attention toward. We'll progress from your hand to a stick, from your stick to a ball and finally use ground targets for moving his body into position and aligning to you from various locations on the field.

Step 1: Place your left hand, palm forward, at a distance of two to three feet from your dog's nose. When he comes forward to sniff your hand, click and reward him immediately.

Step 2: Now add the verbal cue **"<Your dog's name>, Touch!"** Click as his nose touches your hand. Reward him immediately and say **"That'll Do!"** to release your dog.

Step 3: Now move the target (your hand) slightly farther away and repeat the process.

Step 4: Continue to move the target (your hand) to various positions to the front and side and have your dog follow you, clicking as his nose touches your hand and rewarding him immediately. After each repetition, say **"That'll Do!"** to release your dog.

Repeat until your dog has performed the behavior correctly at least four out of five times before moving on to the next level.

Practice this exercise at various times of the day and at varying locations, so that your dog will always move to touch your hand when you ask him. (This behavior is especially useful at your veterinarian's office or at a grooming salon, when trying to get your dog to face forward on a table!)

Exercise 4: Transferring the Touch cue to a target stick

Goal: Your dog will touch his nose to the end of a target stick or any object you direct him to, on cue.

Because your dog will eventually be working at a distance from you, the use of a target stick is recommended. A target stick, painted in high visibility colors (bright blue and bright yellow or red and bright yellow), can be seen better at a greater distance than can a simple hand signal.

Step 1: Place the target stick at a distance of two to three feet from the dog's nose. When your dog comes forward to sniff the end of the stick, click and reward him immediately.

Place the target stick one to two feet away from your dog.

Step 2: Now add the cue **"<Your dog's name>, Touch!"** Click as his nose touches the end of the stick. Reward him immediately and then say **"That'll Do!"** to release him.

Step 3: Continue to move the target stick at different distances in front of the dog. Cue him, saying **"Touch,"** then clicking and rewarding him immediately on each contact as you move. After each successful repetition, say **"That'll Do!"** to release your dog.

Step 4: Transfer the target stick from your left hand to your right, as you did with the hand touch, so that your dog must move 180 degrees (half circle) in an arc in front of you to touch his nose to the end of the stick to earn his click and reward. After each successful repetition, say **"That'll Do!"** to release your dog.

Fin moves left and right touching the target stick on cue.

Repeat until your dog has performed the behavior correctly at least four out of five times before moving on to the next lesson.

Lesson 2

In the Lesson 2 exercises, your dog will learn to orient his body to you in whatever direction you may move. Your dog will learn to line up perpendicular to you as you move to your right or left and also give you direct eye contact when you ask for it. In terms of the handler's position, perpendicular means that we always want the dog to line up with all four legs in a straight line relative to the handler's legs *or* aligned with the handler's spine, so the ball has a straighter trajectory direct to the handler's position within the goal area. If the front legs are aligned with the handler and the back legs are not, when the dog moves the ball, it won't roll in a straight line, and your time will be slower.

The following exercises represent a great opportunity to use pure shaping as a teaching tool. You will simply watch and respond to your dog's movements, and he to yours, as you mark and reward each incremental correct response. Visualize the space in front of you as a clock face. You are standing at the 6 o'clock position with your feet facing your dog. The dog is directly opposite you, at 12 o'clock. As you move around the clock face, you will click and reward your dog each time he lines up perpendicular to you. You may lure the dog into position, if you have to, but only click and deliver the treat when he is lined up directly opposite you. For smaller dogs, use a target stick placed low in his visual range for your dog to focus on more easily.

Don't worry if you dog's progress is slow. You are *shaping* these movements as you go. *Let the clicker speak for you!* You don't need verbal corrections, just wait for him to shift his weight, move his feet or adjust his position. As you move around to reach each position, if your dog does not line up directly opposite you, try shifting your weight slightly from foot to foot. Your dog will most likely shift his weight to match yours, and give you another opportunity to mark and reward the shift. Click and reward each incremental correct step until you get the exact response you want.

If the dog has not completed the movement you're working on, don't reprimand him. Simply don't click. *No click = no reward!* When you click, the dog knows he's done it right and the reward is coming within three to five seconds of completion. The presence or absence of the sound and the reward is all the direction your dog needs. This speaks more strongly to your dog than your voice.

Exercise 1: Your dog will orient his body position to yours as you move clockwise

Step 1: Work with your dog in an enclosed area, off leash with approximately one to two feet of space between you. Cue your dog to make eye contact with you by using the upright hand signal and saying **"<Your dog's name>, Watch me!"**

Step 2: Take a step to your left (to 7 o'clock). As your dog moves directly opposite to face you (to 1 o'clock), click and toss a treat out behind him.

Step 3: Take another step to your left (to 8 o'clock). As your dog comes back to you and moves directly opposite to face you (to 2 o'clock), click and toss a treat out behind him.

Step 4: Take additional steps to your left, one at a time, and pause at each spot where an "hour" marker would be. Click and toss a treat each time your dog comes back to you and adjusts his position to yours as you move around the clock face.

Step 5: When you have both made a complete clockwise rotation, meaning you are back in your original 6 o'clock position and he is in the 12 o'clock position, release him by saying **"That'll Do!"** and take a few steps away.

When your dog is solid (80% reliability) on the full rotation, move on. If your dog is *not* able to make a complete twelve "hour" rotation, break this exercise down into smaller segments by taking larger steps and only move to the quarter-hour marks. *Try the following five steps:*

Step 1: Place your dog standing in front of you with approximately two feet of space between you. Cue your dog to make eye contact with you by using the upright hand signal and saying **"<Your dog's name>, Watch me!"**

Step 2: From your 6 o'clock position, take a big step to your left (to 9 o'clock.) As your dog moves directly opposite to face you (to 3 o'clock), click and toss a treat out behind him.

Step 3: Take another big step to your left (to 12 o'clock.) As your dog moves directly opposite to face you (to 6 o'clock), click and toss a treat out behind him.

Step 4: Now take another big step to your left (to 3 o'clock.) Click and toss a treat out behind him each time he adjusts his position to yours and comes back to line up directly opposite you as you move around the clock face.

Step 5: Now you will step back to the 6 o'clock position where you started, and reward him as he comes back to line up directly opposite you, at 12 o'clock. Click and toss a treat out, then release him by saying **"That'll Do!"** and take a few steps away.

When your dog is solid (80% reliability) on the quarter-hour marks, go back and work on Exercise 1 to make the full 12 hour rotation. When your dog is solid on the full rotation, move on.

Exercise 2: Adding the verbal cue "Line-up" to shape a more exact position

Repeat the above exercise again, with you and your dog moving clockwise, raising the criteria slightly for placement and now adding the verbal cue **"Line-up"** to shape a more exact position.

Step 1: Place your dog standing in front of you with approximately two feet of space between you. Cue your dog to make eye contact with you by using the upright hand signal and saying **"<Your dog's name>, Watch me!"**

Step 2: Take a step to your left (to 7 o'clock). As your dog moves directly opposite to face you (to 1 o'clock) *and if all four of your dog's feet are directly aligned with your knees*, click and toss a treat out behind him. If all four of his feet are not in a direct line with your knees, shift your weight slightly and then hold your position. When he moves into the *best/most correct* position (front feet aligned with his back feet), click and toss a treat out behind him.

Repeat five times, changing your position and clicking and rewarding (shaping) your dog only for the *best/most correct* position. When your dog is lining up directly in front of you, begin to add the verbal cue **"Line-up,"** as you step to the next hour marker.

Step 3: Take another step to your left (to 8 o'clock). As your dog moves directly opposite to face you (to 2 o'clock), wait for him to adjust his position perpendicular to yours. Say **"Line-up,"** and when all four feet are aligned to you, click and toss a treat out behind him.

Step 4: Take additional steps to your left, one at a time, say **"Line-up"** and pause at each spot where an hour marker would be. Click and toss a treat each time your dog comes back to line up directly opposite you as you move around the clock face.

Step 5: When you and your dog have made a complete clockwise rotation, release him by saying **"That'll Do!"** and take a few steps away. Repeat five times, marking and rewarding him when he moves into the *best/most correct* position.

If your dog is not able to make a complete "twelve hour" rotation, break this exercise down into smaller segments by taking larger steps to the quarter-hour marks as was done in Exercise 1.

Step 1: Put your dog on a six foot leash directly in front of you with approximately one to two feet of space between you. Cue your dog to make eye contact with you by using the upright hand signal and saying **"<Your dog's name>, Watch me!"**

Step 2: Say **"Line-up"** and take a big step to your left (to 9 o'clock). As your dog moves directly opposite to face you (to 3 o'clock), click and toss a treat out behind him.

Step 3: Say **"Line-up"** and take another big step to your left (to 12 o'clock). As your dog moves directly opposite to face you (to 6 o'clock), click and toss a treat out behind him.

Step 4: Say **"Line-up"** and take another step to your left (to 3 o'clock). Click and toss a treat each time your dog adjusts his position to yours and then comes back to line up directly opposite you as you move around the clock face.

Step 5: Now you will step back to the 6 o'clock position where you started and reward him as he comes back to line up directly opposite you, at 12 o'clock. Click and toss a treat out, then release him by saying **"That'll Do!"** and take a few steps away.

When your dog is solid (80% reliability) on the quarter-hour marks, go back and work on Exercise 2, adding the cue as you take your steps to make the full twelve hour rotation. When your dog is solid on the full rotation, move on to the next exercise.

Exercise 3: Reverse direction, adding Line-up, with you and your dog moving counterclockwise to your left

Step 1: Work with your dog directly in front of you at 12 o'clock with approximately one to two feet of space between you. Cue your dog to make eye contact with you, by using the upright hand signal and saying **"Watch me!"**

Step 2: Take a step to your right (to 5 o'clock). As your dog moves directly opposite you to the 11 o'clock position, click immediately and toss a treat out behind him. As before, if all four of his feet are *not* in a direct line with your knees, hold your position and simply wait for your dog to shift his stance. When he moves into the *best/most correct* position, click and toss a treat out behind him.

Repeat five times, changing your position and rewarding (shaping) your dog only for the *best/most correct* position.

Step 3: When your dog is lining up directly in front of you, begin to add the cue **Line-up** as you step to the next hour marker. When all four feet are aligned to your knees, click and toss a treat out behind him.

Step 4: Say **"Line-up"** and take additional steps to your right, one at a time. Pause at each spot where an hour marker would be. Each time your dog comes back to line up directly opposite you, click and toss a treat out behind him as you move around the clock face.

Step 5: Mix it up! Play with your dog. Take a step to the right, say **"Line-up"** and then a step to the left, say **"Line-up."** Click and toss out a treat out behind him each time he lines up directly opposite to you! Take two steps left, and then two more. After five repetitions, release your dog by saying **"That'll Do!"** and take a few steps away.

When your dog is solid with 80% reliability on the full rotation, move on.

Lesson 3

Now, for the first time, we introduce the presence of the ball. The goal in this lesson is for your dog to be comfortable moving around the ball without touching it until you give him permission. When he is easily moving around the ball, still orienting his body position perpendicular to you with great eye contact, you allow him to touch the ball with his nose or shoulder and begin to move it forward. In this lesson, we continue to reward the dog at distance by tossing the treat out behind him. By tossing the treat out after the click, you encourage him to come back and realign himself to you as you change your position around the ball.

Exercise 1: Your dog moves clockwise (to your right), and Lines up on cue from behind a ball

For this exercise, your dog should be standing at the 12 o'clock position while you are at the 6 o'clock position. As you step to your left, your dog should orient to you by moving to your right to line up perpendicular to you. You will use the cue **Line-up** before taking a step as you move around the clock face.

Step 1: With the ball between you and your dog, cue him to make eye contact with you by using the upright hand signal and saying **"Watch me!"**

Chance lines up on the opposite side of the ball and watches.

Step 2: Say **"Line-up"** and take a small step to your left (to 7 o'clock), keeping the ball between you and the dog. Wait until all four of his feet are directly perpendicular to your knees. As he moves into direct opposite position (to 1 o'clock) to face you, click and toss a treat out behind him.

Step 3: Move to your next position, a step to your left (at 8 o'clock) and say **"Line-up"** again. As he moves into direct opposite position to face you (to 2 o'clock), click and toss a treat out behind him.

Take a step to your left and treat when the dog positions himself correctly.

Step 4: Move around the ball, stopping at each spot where an hour marker would be. Each time the dog adjusts his position and comes back to line up directly opposite you, click and toss a treat out behind him.

Step 5: When you and your dog have made a complete clockwise rotation around the ball, release him by saying **"That'll Do!"** and take a few steps away.

If your dog finds the ball between you too distracting and cannot make the full twelve hour rotation, go back and break it down into quarter-hour segments as was done earlier so that the exercises move faster. When he is solid with 80% reliability on the quarter-hour markers, move back to Exercise 1 above.

When he is solid in Exercise 1, raise your criteria by only marking and rewarding the best/most correct perpendicular body placement.

Exercise 2: Repeat Exercise 1, but with your dog moving counterclockwise, to your left

Step 1: With the ball between you and the dog, cue your dog to make eye contact with you by using the upright hand signal and saying **"Watch me!"**

Step 2: Say **"<Your dog's name>, Line-up"** and take a step to your right (to 5 o'clock). As he moves into direct opposite position to face you (to 11 o'clock), click and toss a treat out behind him.

Step 3: Take another step to your right (to 4 o'clock). Click and toss a treat out behind him each time he adjusts his position and comes back to line up directly opposite you as you move around the ball.

Step 4: Continue to move, stopping in each spot where an hour marker would be. Click and toss a treat each time the dog adjusts his position and comes back to line up directly opposite you.

Step 5: When your dog has made a complete counterclockwise rotation around the ball, release him by saying **"That'll Do!"** and take a few steps away from the ball.

When he is solid with 80% reliability, repeat again, this time only rewarding for the *best/most correct* perpendicular body placement.

Exercise 3: Using the Touch cue to drive the ball by targeting

Winston targets the midpoint of the ball.

Goal: Your dog will touch his nose to the ball on cue and nudge it forward.

Step 1: Place the ball in front of your feet and move your dog twelve to eighteen inches out behind it.

Step 2: Say **"Line-up"** and wait for your dog to align his position correctly with your knees. Put your hand, palm out, (or the target stick) on the mid-point of the ball and say **"<Your dog's name>, Touch!"**

Step 3: Click as his nose touches your hand, the end of the stick or the ball. Reward him immediately by tossing out a treat behind him and say **"That'll Do!"** to release your dog.

Step 4: Move the ball out two feet, in front of your legs, and place your hand, palm out, (or the target stick) on the mid-point of the ball. Say **"Line-up"** and wait for your dog to align his position correctly with your knees. Add **"<Your dog's name>, Touch!"** and draw your hand or the stick back as you back up a bit.

Step 5: If he nudges your hand, the stick or the ball and it moves forward in any increment, click and reward him by tossing a treat out behind him! If your dog will not move the ball forward from the midpoint with his nose, try hiding a treat under the ball, so he has to nudge it to forward to get the treat. Say **"<Your dog's name>, Touch!"** and click when the ball moves forward.

Chance targets the midpoint and moves the ball forward.

Step 6: Move the ball back to its original position in front of your feet and repeat the process five times. Each time, step back slightly, clicking and rewarding every strong contact with the ball. After the last repetition, say **"That'll Do!"** to release your dog and take a few steps away from the ball.

Joey moves the ball forward by finding a hidden treat.

When practicing Exercise 3 at home, this is the point at which you can begin to raise your criteria. Keep the distance very short between you and the ball, but begin to only click and reward the harder touches, or just reward those touches that occur at or below the midpoint of the ball that move it forward. As your dog gets more adept at moving the ball, you can raise your criteria again and reward only those touches that move the ball forward in a straight line.

Lesson 4

Since it will be necessary for your dog to follow directional cues to gather the ball you choose, he must move left or right according to your signals from your position at the goal. In this lesson we introduce the herding cues **Come Bye!**, and **Away to Me!** to differentiate those movements.

In Treibball, your dog is playing the game facing you, waiting for your instructions. When you ask him to move in any direction, he is moving in relation to you. Using our analogy of the playing field as a clock face, sending your dog to your right from your place at the goal means you will be moving him clockwise. Sending him to your left moves him counterclockwise.

The herding cue **Come Bye!** is short for "Come by the clock," which makes it easy to remember clockwise. The cue **Away to Me!** is used to send your dog in the opposite direction—to your left or counterclockwise. When playing/practicing Treibball, your *right* hand, or the target stick in your right hand, will be used to send the dog clockwise, to your right (his *left*), with **Come Bye!** Your *left* hand, or the target stick in your left hand, will be used to send him counterclockwise to your left (his *right*) with **Away to Me!**

Training tip: If you have trouble remembering which hand matches which cue, take a pair of inexpensive garden gloves, and cut the fingers off at the knuckles. With a permanent marker, mark a big "A" on the top side of your left glove, and a big "C" on the top side of your right glove. Wear these to practice until these cues become automatic.

Exercise 1: Move the dog clockwise to your right (the dog's left) adding the verbal cue, Come Bye!

Try this exercise first with **hand targeting.** The clicker and the leash (if necessary) will be in your left hand. You will use your right hand to bring your dog around an obstacle to his left, and then to a mat that you will place on the field.

Step 1: Your dog is facing you, standing with an obstacle to his left, or your right. You may use a traffic cone, a ball or any obstacle the dog can go around safely. Place the obstacle two feet out, facing you, with the dog's mat directly on the opposite side of the obstacle.

Step 2: Point your feet to the mat and step out slightly on your right foot. Hold your right hand out flat, perpendicular to the obstacle, and move your hand to the right, slowly around the obstacle in a sweeping motion. Say **"<Your dog's name>, Come Bye!"**

Chance will Come Bye! to the mat.

Step 3: Click as he begins to move around the obstacle to confirm that's what you want him to do, and click again when all four of his feet touches the mat. Toss a treat onto the mat. Say **"That'll Do!"** to release your dog and take a few steps away.

Repeat until your dog has performed the behavior correctly at least four out of five times before moving on to the next exercise.

Exercise 2: Step back two feet and repeat Come Bye!, now using the target stick

Chance follows the target stick to Come Bye! to the mat.

The clicker and leash (if necessary) are in your right hand. You will hold the target stick in your right hand and use it to bring your dog around an object to his left and then to the mat.

Step 1: Your dog is standing to the right of a traffic cone or another obstacle with the mat on the opposite side.

Step 2: Point your feet to the mat and step out slightly on your right foot. Hold the target stick out near the middle of the obstacle and move the stick slowly around in a sweeping motion to your right aroundthe obstacle. Say **"<Your dog's name>, Come Bye!"**

Step 3: Click as your dog begins to move around the obstacle and click again when all four of his feet touch the mat. Toss a treat onto the mat to reward him immediately on completion of the move. Say **"That'll Do!"** to release him and take a few steps away.

Chance lies Down on the mat and waits to be released.

Repeat until your dog has performed the behavior correctly at least four out of five times before moving on to the next exercise.

Exercise 3: Move the dog counterclockwise to your left with the verbal cue Away to Me!

Chance is rewarded on the mat after completing the move successfully.

Try this first with hand targeting. The clicker (and leash if necessary) is in your right hand and you use your left hand to bring your dog around the obstacle, to his right, with the mat now on the left (opposite) side of the obstacle.

Step 1: Your dog is on your right side, standing or sitting, standing with a traffic cone or another obstacle to his right (your left), with the mat on the opposite side of the obstacle.

Step 2: Face forward and point your feet toward the mat. Step out slightly on your left foot. Hold your left hand out flat, perpendicular to the obstacle. Move your hand slowly around in a sweeping motion to your left (the dog's right) and say **"<Your dog's name>, Away to Me!"**

Step 3: Click as he begins to move around the obstacle to confirm that's what you wanted and click again when all four of his feet touch the mat. Toss a treat onto the mat to reward him immediately on completion of the move. Say **"That'll Do!"** to release him and take a few steps away.

Repeat until your dog has performed the behavior correctly at least four out of five times before moving on to the next exercise.

Exercise 4: Step back two feet, and repeat Away to Me! now using the target stick

Chance follows the stick to move left with Away to Me!

The clicker and leash (if necessary) are in your right hand. You will hold the target stick in your left hand and use it to bring your dog around an object to his left and then to the mat.

Step 1: Your dog is standing to the right of a traffic cone or another obstacle with the mat on the opposite side.

Step 2: Face forward and point your feet toward the mat. Step out slightly on your left foot. Hold your target stick out, perpendicular to the middle of the obstacle, and move the stick slowly around in a sweeping motion to your left (the dog's right) and say "**<Your dog's name>, Away to Me!**"

Step 3: Click as the dog begins to move around the obstacle and click again when all four of his feet come in contact with the mat. Toss a treat onto the mat. Say **"That'll Do!"** to release him and take a few steps away.

Repeat until you have achieved 80% reliability and then move on to the next exercise..

Exercise 5: Combining Away to Me! and Line-up with Touch when your dog is in place on the mat

The clicker and leash (if necessary) are in your right hand. Hold the target stick in your left hand and use it to bring your dog around the object to his right and then to the mat.

Step 1: Your dog is standing to the right of a traffic cone or another obstacle with the mat on the opposite side.

Step 2: Face forward and point your feet toward the mat. Step out slightly on your left foot. Hold your target stick out, perpendicular to the middle of the obstacle, and move it slowly around in a sweeping motion to your left (and the dog's right) and say **"<Your dog's name>, Away to Me!"**

Step 3: Click as he begins to move around the obstacle and click again when all four of his feet come in contact with the mat. Toss a treat onto the mat.

Step 4: Say **"Line-up"** and wait for him to align his position to yours. When all four of his feet are perpendicular to your knees, click and toss another treat onto the mat.

Step 5: Say **"Touch"** and click when he touches his nose to the end of the stick. Toss a treat onto the mat.

Step 6: Say **"That'll Do!"** to release him and take a few steps away.

Change the position of the mat to the opposite side of the cone and then repeat the exercise using **Come Bye!, Line-up and Touch.** Repeat until you have achieved 80% reliability and then move on to the next lesson.

Lesson 5

After you have sent your dog in the correct direction to gather the ball you've chosen, it's important to have him pause and check in with you. You can do this by having your dog **Stand** behind the designated ball. This gives you another opportunity for making eye contact and also allows you to give him direction before giving the cue to drive the ball forward. As your dog gets faster at playing Treibball, you may decide to have him lie **Down** behind the ball. At the beginner's level, cueing your dog to **Stand** behind the chosen ball keeps the game moving.

Exercise 1: Your dog remains in a Standing position for three to ten seconds, two to three feet from you, and doesn't move until you release him

Chance holds a Stand Stay.

Step 1: Your dog is seated approximately two feet out in front of you. Holding a treat between your thumb and forefinger with your other fingers extended, draw the treat away from his nose directly forward and say **"<Your dog's name>, Stand."**

Step 2: As he moves forward, up onto all four feet, click and treat. Now give him a flat, upright hand signal, adding the verbal cue **Stay**. If at any time you lose his attention, use the upright hand signal, say **"Watch me!"** and continue with your count.

Step 3: Take a step or two back. Hold your position at that distance for a count of three seconds.

Step 4: At the end of your count, step forward. Click again, say **"Take it,"** and allow him to take the treat. Release him by saying **"That'll Do!"** and take a few steps away.

Build up the time your dog will remain in a standing position from three to five seconds, and then from five to seven seconds, then seven to ten before stepping back to him to reward and release him. Practice at each time length until you have achieved five successful completions with 80% reliability before raising your criteria.

Exercise 2: Combining Away to Me! with Stand, Line-up and That'll Do!

Goal: Your dog moves counterclockwise to stand behind the ball and is released on cue.

Step 1: Your dog is facing you. Place a ball twelve to eighteen inches out, between you and your dog, slightly to your dog's right. Place his mat centered directly behind the ball.

Step 2: Step out on your left foot and use your left hand, or the target stick in your left hand, to cue your dog with **Away to Me!** to move him counterclockwise to his right. Click as he begins to move in the correct direction.

Step 3: Click again as he goes directly behind the ball and stands on the mat. Toss a treat onto the mat and give him the cue to **Stand** and **Stay**. If he is not standing perpendicular to you on the mat, say **"Line-up"** and wait for him to align his position to yours.

Step 4: Have him hold that position for a count of ten seconds, then click and treat again, tossing the treat onto the mat in front of him. Release your dog by saying **"That'll Do!"** and take a few steps away.

Repeat until your dog has performed the behavior correctly at least four out of five times before moving on to the next level.

Exercise 3: Combining Come Bye! with Stand/Stay, Line-up and That'll Do!

Goal: Dog moves clockwise to stand behind the ball, lies down and is released on cue.

Step 1: Your dog is facing you. Place a ball twelve to eighteen inches out between you and the dog, slightly to your dog's left. Place his mat directly behind the ball.

Step 2: Step out on your right foot, and use your right hand, or the target stick in your right hand, to cue your dog to **Come Bye!**, moving him clockwise to your right.

Step 3: Click as he goes directly behind the ball and stands on the mat. Toss a treat onto the mat and give him the cue to **Stand** and **Stay**. If he is not standing perpendicular to you on the mat, say **"Line-up"** and wait for him to align his position to you.

Step 4: Have him hold that position for a count of ten seconds, then click and treat again, tossing the treat onto the mat in front of him. Release your dog by saying **"That'll Do!"** and take a few steps away.

Exercise 4: Introducing the Drive! cue by combining it with Touch

Goal: Your dog begins to **Drive!** the ball two to three feet to the goal (you) and then lies **Down** at the goal line

When introducing any new verbal cue, you can first pair it with a cue your dog already knows. As he becomes adept at responding to the new cue, the old one can be dropped or simply used independently. In this exercise we introduce the cue **Drive!**, meaning to actually move the ball forward. Then we combine it with something the dog already knows, **Touch**, meaning to put his nose on the ball.

If you are working on a soft surface (dirt/sand), draw a goal line about four feet long in the sand. If you are working on carpet or indoor flooring, use a strip of masking tape/blue painters tape or something more substantial as your goal line, such as the threshold that transitions from carpet to tile or vinyl flooring. Anything that makes the actual goal line visible to you and that you won't trip on will work.

Step 1: Stand in front of your goal line and place the ball one to two feet out in front of you between you and the dog. Cue your dog to **Stand** and move directly in front the ball or let it rest on the tips of your shoes. Put your target stick on the mid-point or the "equator" of the ball, and then say **"<Your dog's name>, Drive/ Touch."**

Step 2: If the ball moves forward on the **Drive/Touch** cue, click and reward your dog by tossing a treat out behind him, and then back up slightly. If the ball does not move forward, release the dog by saying **"That'll Do!"** Take a few steps away from the ball and begin again.

Click and reward your dog for each touch.

Step 3: Continue to place your stick on the ball and cue your dog with **Drive/Touch** Click and reward him on each touch, rewarding *any* forward motion of the ball by tossing a treat out behind him.

Step 4: If the ball moves forward enough to touch the goal line, cue your dog to lie **Down** immediately. Toss a treat on the ground and say **"That'll Do!"** to release him. Take a few steps away from the ball and begin again.

Step 5: Move back to your original position. Say **"<Your dog's name>, Drive/Touch"** but click only to confirm and reward the stronger contacts with the ball, then toss a treat out behind him.

Step 6: When your dog has moved the ball forward a foot or more with strong contact, cue him to lie **Down** at the goal line. Toss his treat on the ground in front of him and release him, saying **"That'll Do!"** and take a few steps away.

If your dog is showing any stress or reluctance, stop here, reward and release him and come back to these next steps at a later practice session. If he's having fun and is fully engaged with you in driving the ball, continue with the following steps.

Step 7: Move back to your original position and begin again. You will now raise your criteria to mark and reward only those contacts that move the ball forward two feet or more. Use your cue **"<Your dog's name>, Drive/Touch"** but click only to confirm and reward the stronger contacts with the ball, tossing a treat out behind him.

Reward your dog when he can drive the ball at least two feet toward the goal.

Step 8: When your dog has moved the ball with strong contact, two to three feet to the goal line, and lies **Down** on completion, give your dog a *big* reward and then his final release saying **"That'll Do!"** and take a few steps away.

*When your dog is moving the ball forward in 80% of his attempts using the combined cue **Touch/Drive!** drop the **Touch** cue and replace it with **Drive!** alone.*

Training tip: Use pure shaping to encourage your dog to move the ball forward with his nose or shoulder. Give your dog a small target to focus on, by adding a visual marker at the midpoint of the ball. Place a colored Post-It Note™ or use a marker to make an "X" where you want the dog to touch it.

Step 1: Stand in front of your practice goal and place the ball one to two feet out in front of you, between you and the dog, with the visual marker facing the dog. Cue your dog to Stand and Line-up directly behind the ball.

Step 2: If he touches the ball at the target point (the X or Post It) with his nose or shoulder in ANY way, click and reward him immediately by tossing treat out behind him. If he doesn't, release him by saying **"That'll do!"** take a few steps away, and begin again.

Once he makes the connection that putting his nose (or shoulder) on the ball at this small target makes the treat happen, he should make quick progress. Now you can begin to reward him for more accurate touches, or stronger touches that move the ball forward.

Step 3: When he is putting his nose (or shoulder) to the target and moving the ball forward in 80% of his attempts, add the verbal cue. Say **"<Your dog's name> Touch/Drive!"** and reward him on each touch for any forward motion, by tossing a treat out behind him. If the ball comes forward enough to come into the goal, cue your dog to Down immediately. Toss a couple of treats on the ground directly in front of him. Say **"That'll do!"** to release him and take a few steps away.

Step 4: Now raise your criteria. Begin again but click and reward only the stronger contacts with the ball.

More practice suggestions:

- If your dog is hesitant to move the ball forward in an open area, design a practice alleyway. Place some chairs, barstools, or 2 x 6 inch boards spread apart in parallel lines, about the same width as your practice ball.

- Place your dog at the head of the line with the ball in between you.

- Place the target stick or your outstretched hand on the mid-point of the ball and then back up slightly so he must move forward to touch your target stick or your hand.

- Click and reward him on each forward motion of the ball, by tossing a treat behind him (so he must go get the treat and come back to you to line up within the alleyway).

- Click and reward your dog for only the strongest touches or the ones that move the ball the farthest.

Lesson 6

Now that your dog knows which verbal cue matches the desired physical action, you will combine several cues into a continuous, moving behavior, rewarding him only on the completion of the movement.

Exercise 1: Your dog changes direction around the ball, going left and right, with the Come Bye! or Away to Me! cues

Step 1: Designate your goal line by drawing a long line in the sand, behind the ball and in front of your feet, or use masking tape, carpet/tile transition at home so that the goal is visible and your dog can move in a complete 180 degree arc around the ball. Place one ball directly in between you and the dog.

Step 2: With your dog on your left side, or directly in front of you, step off on your right foot and use your right hand, or your target stick in your right hand, saying **"Come Bye!"** to move your dog clockwise around the ball to the far right end of the goal line. Click as he begins to move in the right direction and treat him on the completed move.

Step 3: Now step off on your left foot and use your left hand, or transfer your target stick to your left hand, saying **"Away to Me!"** and move your dog counterclockwise around the ball to the opposite far left end of the goal line. Click as he begins to move in the correct direction and treat him on each completed move.

Step 4: Cue both in succession, alternating sending him right and left. Click each time as the dog begins to move in the correct direction. Treat him on each completed move.

Step 5: After five repetitions, cue him to lie **Down** at the goal line. Click and treat him when he lies **Down**. Release him by saying **"That'll Do!"** and take a few steps away.

Repeat until your dog has achieved 80% reliability, before moving on to the next exercise.

Exercise 2: Combine moving the dog right (using Come Bye!) with Stand/Stay, Line-up and Drive! to move the ball forward six feet to the goal

Goal: Your dog will lie **Down** at the goal line and be released with **That'll Do!**

Step 1: Your dog is standing in front of you, six feet from the goal. Place one ball between you, slightly to the dog's left side. Place your dog's mat behind the ball. Step back to the goal.

Step 2: Step out on your right foot and use your right hand, or the target stick in your right hand, and cue your dog to **Come Bye.** Click as he moves in the correct direction. When he is standing on the mat, directly behind the ball, click again and cue him to **Stand** and **Stay**. If he is not lined up perpendicular to you, use **Line-up** and wait for him to align his position on the mat before adding the next cue.

Step 3: When he is the correct position, say **"<Your dog's name>, Drive!"** (**Touch/Drive!** if you are still using the combined cue).

Step 4: Click each time the ball moves forward. Continue to cue your dog to **Drive!**

Step 5: When the ball reaches you at the goal, click and cue your dog to lie **Down** immediately. Offer him a *big* reward and say **"That'll Do!"** to release him. Take a few steps away from the ball.

Repeat until you have achieved 80% reliability, and then move on to the next exercise.

Exercise 3: Combine moving the dog left, using Away to Me! with Stand and Drive! to move the ball forward six feet to the goal (you). Then Down and That'll Do! at the goal line

Step 1: Your dog is standing in front of you. Cue him to **Stand**, six to eight feet from the goal line. Place one ball between you, slightly to the dog's right side, and step back.

Step 2: Using your left hand, or holding the target stick in your left hand, cue your dog to move left by saying **"Away to Me!"** and click as he moves in the correct direction. When he is standing on the mat, directly behind the ball, click again and cue him to **Stand** and **Stay**. If he is not lined up perpendicular to you, use **Line-up** and wait for him to align his position on the mat before adding the next cue.

Step 3: When he is the correct position, say **"<Your dog's name>, Drive!"** (**Touch/Drive!** if you are still using the combined cue).

Step 4: Click each time the ball moves forward. Continue to cue your dog to **Drive!**

Step 5: When the ball reaches you at the goal line, click and cue your dog to lie **Down** immediately. Offer him a *big* reward and say **"That'll Do!"** to release him. Take a few steps away from the ball.

Repeat until you have achieved 80% reliability before moving on to the next lesson.

Lesson 7

In this lesson, we introduce the concept of the dog backing up in a straight line. This will help him to get behind the correct ball if he overshoots it. After backing up, he will learn how to walk up slowly to position himself behind the ball you've chosen in a direct line to you. Just as live sheep might wander in a pasture, your "sheep" roll out of the direct line to the goal, and under your direction, your dog will need to go back and get them.

Exercise 1: Your dog backs up in a straight line and stays in that position until you direct him to move

Eloise backs up in a straight line.

If your dog already knows a cue for backing up, continue to use that cue. Otherwise, teach your dog the verbal cue **Back**.

Step 1: Place your dog in a **Stand** position between two parallel objects such as 2 x 6 boards, traffic cones or chairs.

Step 2: Step in front of your dog, with the clicker in one hand and a supply of treats in the other. Move forward into your dog's space, flicking your hands toward him at waist level.

Step 3: As he steps back, click to mark each correct step and add the verbal cue **Back**. Reward him for each step backward by tossing a treat out behind him. Allow him to find the treat and then realign himself to you. Repeat, moving into his space and saying **"Back"** on each step. After three to five steps back, say **"That'll Do!"** to release him and take a few steps away.

Step 4: Repeat the exercise and have the dog step back about three to five feet, then five to ten feet while saying **"Back."** Continue to click and reward each step as he moves.

Step 5: When your dog reaches the desired distance, step back to your starting position. Add the verbal cue **Stay** and have him hold that position for a count of ten seconds. At the end of your count, step back to your dog and reward him by tossing a treat out behind him. Say **"That'll Do!"** to release him and take a few steps away.

Repeat until you have achieved 80% reliability, and then move on to the next exercise.

Exercise 2: Reinforcing the Back cue and introducing Walk-on!

Goal: To encourage your dog to approach the ball slowly.

After backing up, Chance will learn to Walk-on! to move forward slowly behind the ball.

Step 1: Place your dog in a **Stand** position, again between two parallel objects. Step in front of your dog with the clicker in one hand and a supply of treats in the other.

Step 2: Move forward into your dog's space, flicking your hands toward him at waist level. As he steps back, click to mark each step away and say **"Back."** Reward him for each step backward by tossing a treat behind him.

Step 3: When your dog reaches the desired distance, step back to your starting position. Hold your hand out at arm's length with the palm facing you and move your fingers forward, or make a larger signal with your entire forearm to encourage your dog to come forward. Say **"Walk-on!"** and click and reward *any* forward movement by tossing a treat out *in front* of him.

Step 4: When your dog reaches you, cue him to **Down** (as you would at the goal line) and reward him. Say **"That'll Do!"** to release him and take a few steps away.

Repeat the exercise and have the dog step back and walk forward, using a distance of three to five feet, then five to ten feet. Continue to click and reward each step as he moves.

Step 5: Raise your criteria now by repeating the exercise, but giving the verbal cues before you give the hand signals or step into his space. Click to mark each step and reward him each time he responds to the verbal cue by taking a step.

Repeat until you have achieved 80% reliability, and then move on to the next exercise.

Exercise 3: Combining Back with Come Bye!, Stand, Drive! and That'll Do!

Chance will Back, Come Bye!, Stand behind the ball, Drive! and then lie Down at the goal.

Step 1: Remove the parallel barriers and place your dog in a **Stand** slightly to your left. Place two balls three to five feet out between you and the dog with one ball slightly behind the other, to the dog's left.

Step 2: Facing your dog, move forward into his space and flick your hands, saying **"Back"** to back him up closer to the balls. Use your right hand, or the target stick in your right hand, to cue him to **Come Bye!** clockwise (to his left) to stand behind the ball placed slightly behind the other.

Step 3: As he goes directly behind the farthest ball, click and cue him to **Stand**. Add the **Touch** or **Drive!** cue, and click and toss him a treat *if* he touches his nose to the ball or moves it forward. If you need to use a cue to move the ball forward again, use **Drive!**

Step 4: When the ball comes forward to you at the goal line, cue your dog to lie **Down**. Reward him *generously* when he lies down in front of you. Release him by saying **"That'll Do!"** and take a few steps away.

Repeat until you have achieved 80% reliability, and then move on to the next exercise.

Lesson 8

Lesson 8 introduces **back-chaining.** This is a technique in which you train a complicated, progressive behavior by repeating each link as an individual action, going backward from the last one to the first, and only rewarding your dog at the end. The dog must complete one more step each time to get the reward. The result is a fluid exercise with multiple cues.

If you lose your dog's attention anytime in this process, use your upright hand signal and say **"Watch me"** before you deliver the next directional cue.

At this point, your dog has learned what verbal cue matches which action, so you may continue to use the target stick, or simply use hand signals and verbal cues to direct him, as he moves left or right, then stations himself behind the ball and moves it to the goal.

Exercise 1: Down and That'll Do!

Step 1: With your dog in a **Sit** or **Stand** in front of the goal line, cue him to lie **Down**.

Step 2: Click on the **Down** and have him hold there for a count of five seconds.

Step 3: At the end of your count, click again and toss a treat to the dog.

Step 4: Say **"That'll Do!"** to release him and take a few steps away from the goal line.

Exercise 2: Drive!, Down and That'll Do!

Step 1: Place a ball one to two feet out from the goal line, directly between you and your dog.

Step 2: Cue your dog by saying **"Drive!"** and click as he moves the ball forward.

Step 3: When the ball comes to the goal line, click and cue your dog to lie **Down**. Click on the **Down** and have him hold there for a count of five seconds.

Step 4: At the end of your count, click again and toss a treat to the dog.

Step 5: Say **"That'll Do!"** to release him and then take a few steps away from the goal line.

Exercise 3: Stand, Drive!, Down and That'll Do!

Step 1: Place a ball one to two feet out from the goal, directly between you and your dog.

Step 2: Place your dog in a **Stand** directly behind the ball. Click on the **Stand** and hold his position there for a count of five seconds.

Step 3: Cue him to **Drive!** and click as he moves the ball forward.

Step 4: As soon as the ball touches the goal line, cue your dog to lie **Down** in front and have him hold that position for a count of five seconds.

Step 5: At the end of your count, click again and toss a treat to your dog. Say **"That'll Do!"** to release him and then take a few steps away from the goal line.

Exercise 4: Back, Stand, Drive!, Down and That'll Do!

Step 1: Place a ball two feet out from the goal line, just slightly off to the side, between you and your dog. Place your dog in a **Stand** directly in front of you.

Step 2: Cue your dog to move **Back** until he is directly behind the ball.

Step 3: Cue him to **Stand** directly behind the ball. Click on the **Stand** and have him hold that position for a count of five seconds.

Step 4: At the end of your count, cue him to **Drive!** Click as he touches his nose to the ball and moves it forward.

Step 5: As soon as the ball touches the goal line, cue your dog to lie **Down** in front and have him hold that position for a count of five seconds.

Step 6: At the end of your count, click again and toss a treat to the dog. Say **"That'll Do!"** to release him and then take a few steps away from the goal line.

Exercise 5: Come Bye!, Stand, Back or Walk-on!, Drive!, Down and That'll Do!

Step 1: Place a ball two feet out from the goal line. Place your dog in a **Sit, Down** or **Stand** on your left.

Step 2: Step out on your right foot and use your right hand, or your target stick, to cue your dog to move to your right with **Come Bye!**

Step 3: Click as your dog moves into place behind the ball. If he is off-center, or overshoots the ball, use the **Back** cue and click on each step backward to line him up directly behind it. If he is too far back behind the ball, cue him to **Walk-on!** and click on each forward step until he is aligned directly behind it.

Step 4: When he is positioned directly behind the ball, cue him to **Stand**. Click on the **Stand** and have him hold that position for a count of five seconds.

Step 5: At the end of your count, cue your dog to **Drive!** and click as the ball moves forward.

Step 6: As soon as the ball touches the goal line, cue your dog to lie **Down** in front and have him hold that position for a count of five seconds.

Step 7: At the end of your count, click and toss a treat to your dog. Say **"That'll Do!"** to release him and then take a few steps away from the goal line.

Exercise 6: Away to Me!, Stand, Back or Walk-on!, Drive!, Down and That'll Do!

Step 1: Place a ball two feet out from the goal. Place your dog in a **Stand** on your right.

Step 2: Step out on your left foot and use your left hand, or your target stick, to cue him to move to your left with **Away to Me!**

Step 3: Click as your dog moves into place behind the ball. If he is off-center, or overshoots the ball, use the **Back** cue and click on each step back to line him up directly behind it. If he is too far back behind the ball, cue **Walk-on!** and click on each forward step until he is aligned directly behind it.

Step 4: When he is positioned directly behind the ball cue him to **Stand**. Click on the **Stand** and have him hold there for a count of five seconds.

Step 5: At the end of your count, cue your dog to **Drive!** and click as he moves the ball forward.

Step 6: As soon as the ball touches the goal line, cue your dog to lie **Down** in front and have him hold that position for a count of five seconds.

Step 7: At the end of your count, click and *give your dog a jackpot!!!* Say **"That'll Do!"** to release him and then take a few steps away from the goal line.

Whew! Congratulations! Now you're ready to play Treibball.

Lesson 9

Setting up a practice game for fun

So far, you've taught your dog how to target the ball. He knows to watch you for the directional cues to have him move right or left. He knows how to move forward or to back up, how to hold a position by standing behind the ball, how to drive the ball directly to you when given the cue to do so, and to lie down and wait to be released at the goal line.

Now you can practice playing Treibball with real timing, but not real distance. Work only with the number of balls you and your dog are comfortable with. *Remember, this is supposed to be fun!* You can always add more balls and/or increase the playing distance to the goal as your teamwork becomes more proficient.

Izzie stands ready to play.

Set up: Use an area fifteen to twenty feet long and at least ten to twelve feet wide.

Create a goal large enough to hold three to eight balls. You can use your dog's exercise pen with two sections/arms extended, or create any area that has an obvious opening with the ends blocked off.

Place the ball-set ten feet out from the goal. Arrange the balls in a triangle shape, with the longest line of balls facing the goal and the point ball farthest from the goal line.

- **Arrangement for three balls:** Place two balls in front and the point ball directly centered behind them.

- **Arrangement for six balls:** Place three balls in front, two behind them and the point ball directly centered behind the two.

- **Arrangement for eight balls:** Place four balls in front, three behind them and the point ball centered behind the three.

Use a stopwatch or an oven timer, or enlist the aid of a friend to be your timekeeper.

Depending on your space constraints, you can begin one of two ways. If you're using a wide space, begin by cueing your dog to **Stand** and **Stay** to your left of the ball-set. In a narrower space, begin by cueing him to **Stand** and **Stay** directly behind the point ball.

To begin have your dog stand behind the balls, ten feet away from you and the goal.

Set your timer for ten minutes, or have your timekeeper signal you to start.

At the start of timing, cue your dog to **Drive!** the point ball to you. Use your directional cues to adjust his position and send him left or right, depending on which way the first ball rolls. If he overshoots the ball, use the **Back** cue to get him back in a straight line behind the ball. If you need to move him slowly forward, use **Walk-on!**

As the ball-set is broken up and each ball is driven to the goal line, click and toss a treat behind your dog, before sending him out with new directions to bring in the next ball.

When all the balls are in the goal, or when your timekeeper calls time, cue your dog to lie **Down** and offer him a *big* reward (a jackpot). Then release him by saying **"That'll Do!"** and take a few steps away.

Once your dog is lying down calmly, give him a jackpot!

Now simply practice and have some fun with it. As Mr. Nijboer originally stated, it's not just about how many balls are in the goal, it's about stronger teamwork between you and your dog!

After your fundamental communications skills have been strengthened by practice and these new cues are solid, you can add more balls and increase your dog's control at a distance. That's the focus of the Intermediate lessons that follow in which you add more balls and continue to build your dog's focus as you increase the distance between you and the dog.

4

Intermediate Treibball Training

In the Introductory Treibball curriculum, you taught your dog the verbal cues and the matching movements used to play Treibball. The Intermediate Level section teaches you how to build your dog's reliability at a distance from the goal and to improve your dog's skill at moving multiple balls to you.

Like the previous lessons, these are also progressive. Each exercise builds on the preceding one, using shaping as the primary training technique. You will begin, as before, with a rapid rate of reinforcement, rewarding the dog for every correct execution. As your dog becomes more accomplished at moving multiple balls at greater distances, you will raise your criteria to reward him only on the completion of the movement or task, or to reward him for the best execution of that task. As you vary the rate of reward, begin to substitute any of the verbal markers your dog knows, such as **"Wait"** or **"Watch me"** as your **"Keep going"** signal and fade the use of the click.

Building your dog's reliability and attention to you at a substantial distance is a skill that can be used in a variety of situations and environments, including in an emergency where your dog's safety is at stake. At this level, Treibball becomes both a fun game and, the more you play, a vehicle for even stronger communication between the two of you. Diagrams of the more complex exercises have been added for clarity.

The lessons and exercises included in this section are as follows:

- Lesson 1
  - Stand/Stay at an increasing distance
  - Down/Stay at ten to twenty feet
  - Increasing distance for directional cues, moving left
  - Increasing distance for directional cues, moving right

- Lesson 2
  - Move out to target, then Stand/Stay and Down
  - Introduce (Go) Out cue and pair it with directional cues
  - (Go) Out to ball ten to fifteen feet away
  - Use all cues in combination to drive the ball
  - Reverse position of cone, Stand/Watch Drive

- Lesson 3
  - Down/Stay fifteen feet from goal line
  - (Go) Out/Away to Me! around two to three balls
  - Introduce a second starting point
  - Move from Down to starting position then adding directional cues to drive balls

- Lesson 4
  - Positioning exercise for better ball control
  - Start/(Go) Out to move three to five balls to goal
  - Start right, move to left, drive three to five balls to goal

- Lesson 5
  - (Go) Out/Come Bye! then Stand on Cue and wait for release.
  - (Go) Out/Come Bye! then Stand on Cue then drive five balls to goal

- Lesson 6
  - Set up practice field with full set of eight balls using official distance and timing. Dog is able to drive all balls to the goal as in match play.

Ready, set, let's go!

Lesson 1

With this lesson, you begin to build your dog's ability to take direction at a distance. As with any behavior, you start out at close range and increase your distance in manageable increments. You begin by asking the dog to **Stand** and **Stay** and to **Down** and **Stay** to position him better behind the ball.

Until you have complete control of your dog's movements within the playing field, you will be cueing him to **Stand** behind the ball you have chosen for him to bring forward. As he becomes faster at moving the ball to the goal, you may choose to have him lie **Down** behind each selected ball. If he gets too excited about herding the balls, having him **Stand** and **Watch** or lie **Down** behind the ball to pause the action and allow you to redirect his attention to you.

Exercise 1: Your dog will Stand/Stay at an increasing distance from you (five to ten feet) and be released with That'll Do!

Aedan holds a Stand/Stay at ten feet and Watches.

Step 1: Use your hand signal and the verbal cue for your dog to **Stand**. As he moves forward, click but do not treat.

Step 2: Transfer the treat to your right hand and give him a flat hand signal with your left hand, adding the verbal cue **Stay**.

Step 3: Back up five feet. Hold your position for a count of five seconds.

Step 4: At the end of your count, return to your dog, click again and toss a treat to him. Say **"That'll Do!"** to release him and take a few steps away.

Step 5: Now begin again. Cue him to **Stand**. As he moves forward, click but do not treat.

Step 6: Transfer the treat to your right hand and give him a flat hand signal with your left hand, adding the verbal cue **Stay**.

Step 7: Back up ten feet. Hold your position there for a count of five seconds.

Step 8: At the end of your count, return to your dog, click again and toss the treat to him. Say **"That'll Do!"** for release and take a few steps away.

Begin with your dog standing and staying for five seconds at ten feet away, then build up to a **Stay** of fifteen to thirty seconds at ten feet away before rewarding and releasing him. Repeat until you have achieved 80% reliability at ten feet before raising your criteria in five foot increments, to fifteen and then twenty feet.

Exercise 2: Down/Stay at ten to twenty feet and release at a distance

Kita holds a Down/Stay at ten feet from the goal.

Goal: Your dog will lie Down and Stay at an increasing distance from you and be released with That'll Do!

Step 1: With your dog in front of you, give him the verbal and visual cues to **Sit** and then to lie **Down** and **Stay**. Step back five feet.

Step 2: If he remains in place, hold your position for a count of ten to fifteen seconds. You may continue to use the hand signal, but do not repeat the verbal cue.

Step 3: If he gets up, step back to him and put him back into position.

Step 4: If he has remained in position after your count, return to your dog. Click, toss the treat to him, say **"That'll Do!"** for release, and take a few steps away.

Begin again, now increasing the distance between you and your dog.

Step 1: With your dog in front of you, give him the verbal and visual cues to **Sit**, **Down** and **Stay** as before, then step back another five feet. Again, you may continue to use the hand signal, but do not repeat the verbal cue.

Step 2: Hold your position there for a count of ten to fifteen seconds.

Step 3: If he has remained in position after your count, return to him. Click and toss the treat to him, say **"That'll Do!"** for release and take a few steps away.

Repeat until you have achieved 80% reliability at ten feet before raising your criteria in five foot increments, to fifteen and then twenty feet.

Exercise 3: Increasing the distance for the directional cues by moving left with Away to Me! at a minimum distance of three to five feet from you

Eloise moves left with Away to Me! around the obstacles to the mat.

Step 1: Your dog is standing to your right of a traffic cone or a ball, with you standing in front of the ball or the cone, at a distance of three feet out. Place your dog's mat behind the obstacle as a visual target.

Step 2: Step out on your left foot and use your left hand, or your target stick in your left hand, to cue the dog to move to your left, saying **"Away to Me!"**

Step 3: Click as he begins to move around the obstacle and, as he moves, back up two feet. Reward him immediately upon completion of the move by tossing a treat onto the mat.

Step 4: Say **"That'll Do!"** to release him and take a few steps away.

Repeat until you have achieved 80% reliability at ten feet before raising your criteria in five foot increments, to fifteen and then twenty feet.

Exercise #4: Increasing the distance for the directional cues by moving the dog to your right with Come Bye!, at a minimum distance of three to five feet from you

Step 1: Your dog is standing to your left of a traffic cone or the ball, with you standing in front of the ball or the cone, at a distance of three feet. Place your dog's mat behind the obstacle as a visual target

Step 2: Step out on your right foot and use your right hand, or the target stick in your right hand, to cue your dog to move to your right around the obstacle to the mat. Say **"<Your dog's name>, Come Bye!"**

Step 3: Click as he begins to move around the obstacle and then back up two feet. Reward him immediately on the completion of the move by tossing a treat out onto the mat.

Step 4: Say **"That'll Do!"** to release your dog and take a few steps away.

Repeat until you have achieved 80% reliability at ten feet before raising your criteria in five foot increments, to fifteen and then twenty feet.

Lesson 2

In this lesson, you continue combining each directional cue into a complete fluid movement, and then build up the distance between you from six to ten feet while still maintaining your dog's attention. You will also introduce the **(Go) Out!** cue for increasing your dog's distance from the goal.

If your dog competes in agility or is already familiar with the cue **Go Out** or **Out** for an outrun, continue to use that term. If you have another cue or term your dog is familiar with, use *that* term. If you have not used a cue like this before, introduce **Out** at this time and pair it with the correct directional cue to send your dog farther away from you.

Just as we paired **Touch** with **Drive!** in Lesson 3 of the Introductory section, when introducing any new verbal cue, it's important to say the new cue directly before the cue that your dog already knows. Pairing the new cue with one your dog already knows aids in linking these behaviors together. Once the dog understands the meaning and is complying with your new cue 80% of the time, you may begin to fade the second cue or use both cues independently of each other.

Exercise 1: Your dog moves out six feet to a target (his mat) using the cues Come Bye! and Away to Me!, then orients to you with Watch me, and then will Stand/Stay and Down on the mat and wait for release with That'll Do!

Chance will Come Bye! around the cones and balls and then hold a Stand/Stay on the mat.

Chance will move Away to Me! around the cones and balls and hold a Stand/Stay on the mat.

Note: You (the handler) do not step into the field.

Lesson #2
Exercise #1

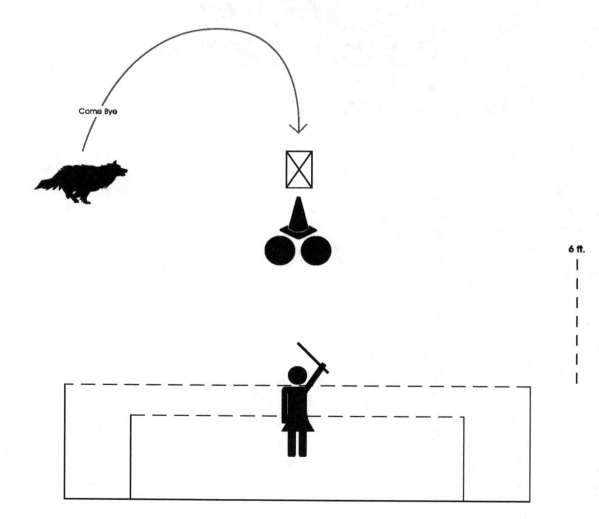

Come Bye

6 ft.

Step 1: Fold your dog's mat into a smaller target (one to two square feet), and place it out three feet in front of you, six feet from the goal. Place one or more balls and a cone or other obstacles directly in front of the mat. With your dog on your left side in a heel position, step out on your right foot and use your right hand, or the target stick in your right hand, to send your dog to your right, out around the obstacles to the mat. Say **"<Your dog's name>, Come Bye!"**

Step 2: Click as he moves around the obstacles and click again when all four of his feet come in contact with the mat. Toss a treat onto the mat. If you like, cue your dog to **Stand/Stay** on the mat.

Step 3: Use your upright hand signal to focus his attention and say **"Watch me!"** Click immediately on eye contact and toss a treat onto the mat.

Step 4: Cue your dog to lie **Down** on the mat. Hold his position there for a count of five to ten seconds. At the end of your count, click and then toss a few treats onto the mat.

Step 5: Say **"That'll Do!"** to release your dog and take a few steps away.

Now repeat the exercise with **Away to Me!**

Step 1: Now with your dog standing on your right side, step out on your left foot and use your left hand, or the target stick in your left hand, to send your dog to your left out and around the obstacles to the mat. Say **"<Your dog's name>, Away to Me!"**

Step 2: Click as he moves around the obstacles and click again when all four of his feet come in contact with the mat. Toss a treat onto the mat. If you like, cue your dog to **Stand/Stay** on the mat.

Step 3: Use your upright hand signal to focus his attention and say **"Watch me!"** Click immediately on eye contact, and toss a treat onto the mat.

Step 4: Now cue your dog to lie **Down** on the mat. Hold his position there for a count of five to ten seconds. At the end of your count, click and then toss a few treats onto the mat.

Step 5: Say **"That'll Do!"** to release your dog and take a few steps away.

Repeat both sequences (**Come Bye!** and **Away to Me!**) until your dog has achieved 80% reliability at six feet before raising your criteria.

Exercise 2: As you now increase the distance from six to ten feet to the target, you introduce the (Go) Out! cue and pair it with the directional cues your dog already knows

You will move your dog to your right using **Come Bye!** and to your left with **Away to Me!**, then cueing a **Stand** directly behind the ball at a minimum ten to fifteen feet distance from you, releasing him with **"That'll Do!"**

Izzie backs up to get positioned directly behind the balls.

Izzie Stands and Watches on the mat behind the obstacles.

You (the handler) do not step into the field.

Step 1: Place your dog's mat ten feet out from you with one or more balls directly in front of the mat and a cone blocking the access at the near left-front corner of the mat.

Step 2: With your dog standing to your left, step out on your right foot and use your right hand signal or your target stick in your right hand to send your dog out to your right around the obstacles to the mat. Say **"<Your dog's name >, (Go) Out!/Come Bye!"**

Step 3: Click as he moves around the obstacles and click again when all four of his feet come in contact with the mat. Toss a treat onto the mat.

Step 4: If he is not aligned properly and you need to reposition him, use **Back** or **Walk-on!** combined with the **Come Bye!** or **Away to Me!** until the dog is correctly positioned on the mat.

Step 5: When he lines up correctly, use your upright hand signal and say **"Watch me!"** before giving a further cue. Click immediately on eye contact and then cue him to **Stand** on the mat.

Step 6: Walk up to your dog, click and toss a treat onto the mat. Say **"That'll Do!"** to release him and take a few steps away.

Repeat until your dog has achieved 80% reliability at ten feet before raising your criteria. When he is moving reliably to your right behind the obstacles to stand on the mat/target, step back another five feet and repeat until he reliably stations on the mat behind the obstacles fifteen feet or more from the goal.

Lesson #2
Exercise #2

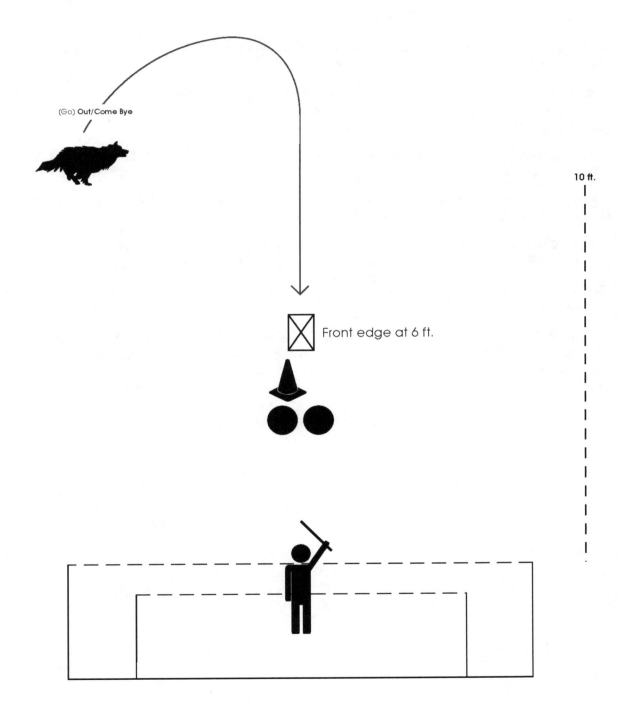

Exercise 3: Repeat, now combining (Go) Out! with Away to Me! You are moving your dog to your left using (Go) Out!/Away to Me!, repositioning him with Back or Walk-on!, then cueing a Stand directly behind the ball at a minimum of ten to fifteen feet distance from you, and releasing him with "That'll Do!"

You (the handler) do not step into the field.

Step 1: Keep the mat and balls in position but reverse the placement of the cone and begin again. Place the cone blocking the access at the near right-front corner of the mat.

Step 2: With your dog standing on your right side in the heel position, step out on your left foot and use your left hand signal or the target stick in your left hand, to send your dog to your left around the obstacles to the mat. Say **"<Your dog's name>,** (Go) **Out!/Away to Me!"**

Step 3: Click as he moves around the obstacles and click again when all four of his feet come in contact with the mat. Toss a treat onto the mat.

Step 4: If he is not aligned properly and you need to reposition, use the **Back** or **Walk-on!** cue or another **Come Bye!** or **Away to Me!** until he is correctly positioned on the mat.

Step 5: When he lines up correctly, use your upright hand signal and say **"Watch me!"** before giving a further cue. Click immediately on eye contact and then cue him to lie **Down** or **Stand** on the mat.

Step 6: Walk up to your dog, click and toss a treat onto the mat. Say **"That'll Do!"** to release him and take a few steps away.

Repeat until your dog has achieved 80% reliability at ten feet. When he is moving reliably to your left behind the obstacles to stand on the mat/target, step back another five feet and repeat until he reliably stands on the mat behind the obstacles fifteen feet or more from the goal line.

Lesson #2
Exercise #3

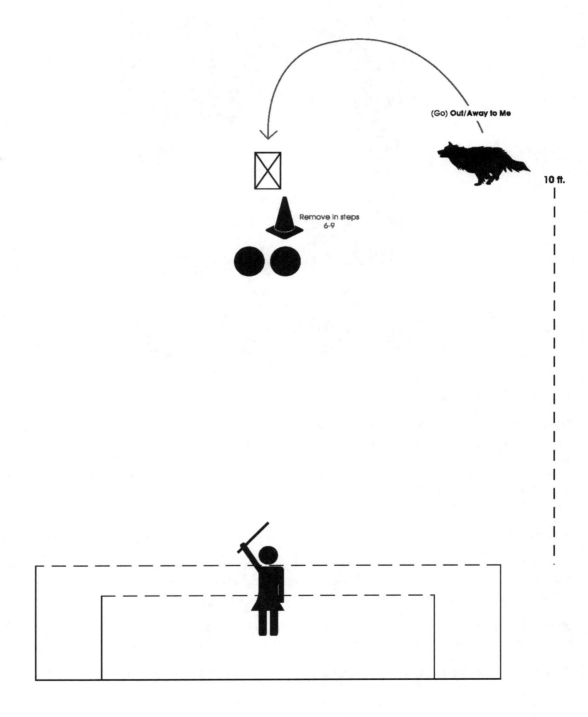

(Go) Out/Away to Me

Remove in steps
6-9

10 ft.

Exercise 4: Now reverse the position of the cone and repeat, with the dog standing on your right. Your dog will (Go) Out!, move to your left with Away to Me!, Stand on the mat, Watch and then Drive one ball, from ten feet out, to you at the goal.

Eloise targets the midpoint of the ball and Drives!

Eloise drives the ball to the goal.

You (the handler) do not step into the field.

Step 1: Place the mat ten feet out from the goal with one or more balls directly in front of the mat and a cone blocking the access at the near left-front corner of the mat.

Step 2: With your dog standing to your left, step out on your right foot and use your right hand signal, or the target stick in your right hand, to send your dog out to your right, around the obstacles to the mat. Say **"<Your dog's name >**, (Go) **Out!/Come Bye!"**

Step 3: Click as he moves around the obstacles and click again when all four of his feet come in contact with the mat, then toss a treat onto the mat.

Step 4: When he is positioned properly behind one ball, use your upright hand signal and say **"Watch me!"** If he overshoots the ball, use **Back**, and if he needs to move up closer use **Walk-on!**

Step 5: Add the **Stand** (or **Stand/Stay**) cue to keep him in position directly behind the ball. Walk up to the mat and remove the cone from the right front corner of the mat. Step back to your position at the goal line.

Step 6: Cue your dog to **Drive!** and click on each forward movement of the ball until it reaches your feet.

Step 7: Give your dog a big reward when the ball reaches you! Cue him to lie **Down** at the goal and say **"That'll do!"** to release him. Now take a few steps away from the goal area.

Repeat until your dog has achieved 80% reliability at ten feet. When he is moving reliably to your right behind the obstacles to stand on the mat and bringing one ball to the goal, move the mat and obstacles five feet farther out from the goal. When your dog has achieved 80% reliability at fifteen feet, add more balls or increase your distance.

Exercise 5: Now, reverse the position of the cone and repeat with the standing dog on your right. Your dog will (Go) Out!, move left with Away to Me!, Stand on the mat, Watch and Drive! one ball from ten feet out, to you at the goal.

You (the handler) do not step into the field.

Step 1: Place the mat ten feet out with one or more balls directly in front of the mat and a cone blocking the access at the near right-front corner of the mat.

Step 2: With your dog in **Stand** on your right side in the heel position, step out on your left foot and use your left hand signal or the target stick in your left hand, to send your dog out around to your left, around the obstacles to the mat. Say **"<Your dog's name>, (Go) Out!/Away to Me!"**

Step 3: Click as the dog moves around the obstacles and click again when all four of his feet come in contact with the mat, then toss a treat onto the mat.

Step 4: When he is positioned properly behind one ball, use your upright hand signal and say **"Watch me!"** If he overshoots the ball, use the **Back** cue, and if he needs to move up closer, use **Walk-on!**

Step 5: Add the **Stand** (or **Stand/Stay**) cue to hold his position directly behind the ball. Walk up to the mat and remove the cone from the front corner of the mat. Step back to your position at the goal line.

Step 6: Cue your dog to **Drive!** and click on each forward movement of the ball until it reaches your feet. Give your dog a *BIG* reward when the ball reaches you!!

Step 7: Cue your dog to lie down at the goal, and say **That'll do!** to release him. Now take a few steps away.

Repeat until your dog has achieved 80% reliability at ten feet. When he is moving reliably to your left behind the obstacles to stand on the target and bringing one ball to the goal, move your mat and obstacles five feet farther out from the goal. When your dog has achieved 80% reliability at fifteen feet, vary the exercise by adding more balls or increasing your distance (but not both at once, please!!)

Lesson 3

In this lesson, you replace your dog's usual mat with a smaller visual target behind the balls and introduce another flat target to be used as the starting point. Similar to his mat, a smaller target that you and your dog can both see can make his eventual placement at the start position behind the point ball more correct and precise. Use a material that is thin and non-slip, something comfortable for your dog to stand on, in a contrasting color or texture from the flooring of your training area.

An assortment of easy, flat ground targets: A plastic drain cover,
vinyl shelf sheeting, thin yoga matting and foam flooring piece.

By asking your dog to look for and hit his target, you are strengthening his spatial control and reinforcing proper body positioning (for **Stand** or **Down**) before driving the ball. Your dog should be able to move left with **Away to Me!** or right with **Come Bye!**, remain in a **Stand** or **Down** behind the ball, and make eye contact with you before being released.

Exercise 1: Your dog holds a Down/Stay at a distance of fifteen feet from the goal line

Aeden holds a Down/Stay on a small target fifteen feet from the goal.

Step 1: Place one target on the ground directly in front of you, fifteen feet from the goal. If you wish, you may place balls/obstacles directly in front of the target.

Step 2: Walk your dog out to the target and then use your verbal and hand signals to cue him to lie **Down**. Click on the **Down**. Toss a treat on the ground near the target and then add your verbal or hand signal for **Stay**.

Step 3: Step back fifteen feet to the goal line and hold your position there for a count of ten to fifteen seconds. You can repeat the hand signal, but try not to repeat the verbal cue.

Step 4: At the end of your count, return to your dog and click, then toss a treat on the ground near the target. Say **"That'll Do!"** to release him and take a few steps away.

Repeat until your dog has reached 80% reliability before increasing the criteria for time or distance. Build up to 80% reliability for ten to fifteen seconds at 20 to 30 feet.

Repeat the above exercise now using **Stand/Stay** at a distance of fifteen feet from the goal line.

Eloise moves to a Stand/Stay on the mat at fifteen feet from the goal.

Step 1: Place one target on the ground directly in front of you, fifteen feet from the goal. If you wish, you may place balls/obstacles directly in front of the target.

Step 2: Walk your dog out to the target, then use your verbal and hand signals to cue him to **Stand**, then add your verbal or hand signal for **Stay**.

Step 3: Step back fifteen feet and hold your position there for a count of ten to fifteen seconds. You can repeat the hand signal, but try not to repeat the verbal cue.

Step 4: At the end of your count, return to your dog and click, then toss a treat on the ground near the target. Say **"That'll Do!"** to release him and take a few steps away.

Repeat until your dog has reached 80% reliability before increasing the criteria for time or distance. Build up to 80% reliability for a **Stand/Stay** of ten to fifteen seconds at 20 to 30 feet.

Exercise 2: Use (Go) Out!/Away to Me! to move left around two to three balls to a target, and use (Go) Out!/Come Bye! to move right around two or three balls to a target at a distance of ten to fifteen feet from the goal line between you and the goal

Place two to three balls or cones in the field between you and your dog, ten to fifteen feet from the goal line. Place your ground target directly behind the balls/obstacles. Your dog is standing to your right (his left) of the balls/obstacles.

Step 1: Stand at the goal line and cue your dog to make eye contact with you by saying **"Watch me!"**

Step 2: Click on eye contact, then step out on your left foot and use your left hand, or your target stick in your left hand, to send him to your left around the balls/cone to the target. Say **"<Your dog's name> then (Go) Out!/ Away to Me!"**

Step 3: Click as he moves to your left around the obstacles, and click again when all four of his feet come into contact with the target behind them.

Step 4: Use your verbal and hand signal **Stand/Stay** cues to keep your dog in position there for a count of ten to fifteen seconds.

Step 5: At the end of your count, return to him. Click to mark the Stand/Stay and then toss a treat on the ground near the target. Say **"That'll Do!"** immediately to release him and take a few steps away.

Repeat until your dog has performed the behavior with 80% reliability before increasing the criteria for distance or time.

Lesson #3
Exercise #2

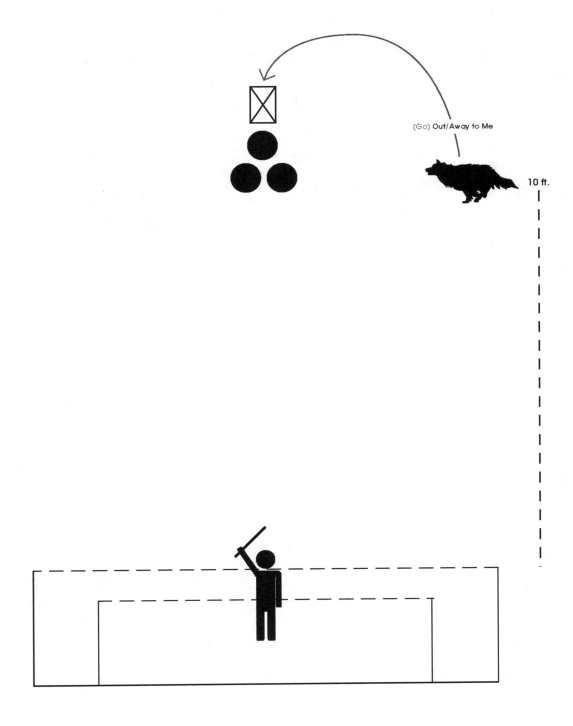

(Go) Out/Away to Me

10 ft.

Repeat with Come Bye!

Place two to three balls or cones in the field at a distance of ten to fifteen feet from the goal line between you and your dog. Place a ground target directly behind the balls/obstacles. Your dog is standing to your left (his right) of the balls/obstacles.

Step 1: Stand at the goal line and cue your dog to make eye contact with you by saying **"Watch me!"**

Step 2: Click immediately on eye contact, then step out on your right foot and use your right hand, or your target stick in your right hand, to send him around the balls/cones. Say **"<Your dog's name>, (Go) Out!/Come Bye!"**

Step 3: Click on the correct movement as he moves around the obstacles and click again when all four of his feet come into contact with the target behind them.

Step 4: Use your verbal and hand signal **Stand/Stay** cues to keep your dog in position there for a count of ten to fifteen seconds.

Step 5: At the end of your count, return to your dog. Click to mark the **Stand/Stay** and then toss a treat on the ground near the target. Say **"That'll Do!"** to release him and take a few steps away.

Repeat until your dog has performed the behavior with 80% reliability five times before increasing the criteria for distance or time.

Exercise 3: Introduce a second target at the starting point in addition to the one already placed behind the balls/obstacles

Kita lies Down in the Start position and watches for her cue.

In this exercise, your dog is walked out to the starting target and placed in a **Down/Stay.** He then orients to you with **Watch me!** before being sent to (Go) **Out!** and **Come Bye!** to the second target behind the obstacles. Your dog will **Stand** and **Stay** on the target until released with **That'll Do!** To begin, place two to three balls or cones in the field, at a distance of fifteen feet from the goal, between you and your dog. A ground target is placed directly behind the balls/obstacles. Another small target is placed at your left, at the 10 o'clock position, relative to the target behind the balls (which would be at 12 o'clock).

Step 1: With your dog on your left side, step out with your left foot and use the verbal cue you normally use for loose leash walking, such as **Heel** or **Let's go.** When you reach the first target to your left, in the 10 o'clock position, place your dog in a **Down**. Click on the **Down** and toss a treat onto the ground.

Step 2: Use your hand signal and the verbal cue **Stay**. Return to your position at the goal. When you reach the goal line, turn to face your dog. Say **"Watch me!"** to have him give you his attention before sending him out behind the balls.

Step 3: Step out on your right foot and use your right hand, or the target stick in your right hand, to move him to your right, around the obstacles to the target. Say **"<Your dog's name>, (Go) Out!/Come Bye!"**

Step 4: Click when his feet come in contact with the target. Say **"Watch me!"** to have him focus on your face for the next cue. Click immediately when he makes eye contact with you.

Step 5: Use your hand signal and the verbal cue to have your dog **Stand/Stay** on the target. Hold his position there for a count of ten to fifteen seconds.

Step 6: At the end of your count, walk up to where your dog is standing on the target. Click and reward him generously. Say **"That'll Do!"** for release and take a few steps away.

Repeat until your dog has performed the behavior correctly at least four out of five times increasing the criteria for distance or time.

Exercise 4: Your dog moves from a Down at the starting position, orients to you with Watch me!, then moves down-field with (Go) Out!, moves right with Come Bye!, or left with Away to Me!, to Stand on the target behind the balls and drives one to three balls ten feet to you at the goal

Set for Come Bye! One ball and two targets.

Set for Come Bye! Three balls and two targets.

Set for Away to Me! One ball and two targets.

Set for Away to Me! Three balls and two targets.

Lesson #3
Exercise #4

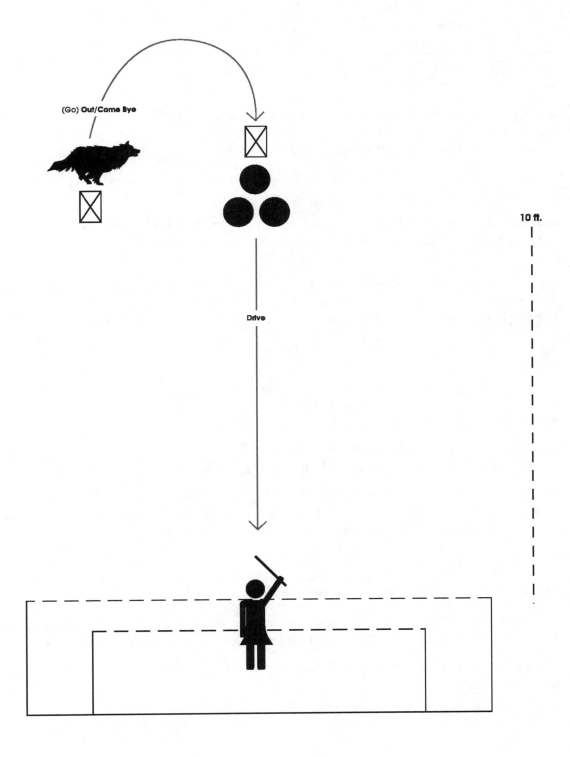

To use our clock-face analogy, you are standing at the goal in the 6 o'clock position. On your cue your dog will move from the target placed at 10 o'clock to **Come Bye!** and **Stand** on the target placed at 12 o'clock. He will then move left or right, line up perpendicular to the selected ball and drive all the balls to you at the goal line.

Place one to three balls mid-field, ten feet from the goal line. If you choose to work with three balls, place them in a triangle formation with a peak/point ball behind the two balls in front. Place one small target to the left of the front two balls (or single ball) at the 10 o'clock position, and the other larger ground target directly behind the point ball. If you're using a single ball, place one target to the left of the ball and one target directly behind it.

Step 1: With your dog on your left side, use your loose leash walking cue and walk your dog out to the starting target on your left. When you reach the target, place your dog in a **Down**. Click on the **Down** and toss a treat onto the ground near the target.

Step 2: Use your verbal and hand signal for **Stay** and return to your position in front of the goal. Face your dog. Step out on your right foot and use your right hand, or the target stick in your right hand, to send your dog to your right. Say "**<Your dog's name>,** (Go) **Out!/Come Bye!**"

Step 3: If he overshoots the ball, use the **Back** cue. If he needs to move forward, use **Walk-on!** to have him move up to the ball slowly.

Step 4: Click to confirm as he moves to your right (his left) and click again when he comes into contact with the target behind the balls. Say "**Watch me!**" to cue him to make eye contact. Click immediately when his eyes make contact with yours.

Step 5: Cue him to **Stand** on the target and click to confirm when he assumes that position. If necessary, say "**Line-up**" until he is directly perpendicular to the ball. When he lines up opposite you or stands directly behind the point ball, say "**Drive!**" Click on each forward motion of the ball until it reaches you at the goal line.

Step 6: Reward your dog with several treats for bringing the ball to your feet and then cue your dog to lie **Down** at the goal line.

Step 7: Say "**That'll Do!**" to release your dog and take a few steps away from the goal.

If you are working with three balls, continue the exercise as follows:

Step 8: Step off on your left foot and use your left hand, or the target stick in your left hand, to send him out to your left (his right) behind the remaining ball(s). Say "**<Your dog's name>,** (Go) **Out!/Away to Me!**"

Step 9: If he overshoots the ball, use the **Back** cue. If he needs to move forward, use **Walk-on!** to have him move up slowly. When he is lined up perpendicular to your choice of the remaining balls, click to confirm that he is correct and then cue him to **Drive!** until that ball reaches you at the goal line.

Step 10: Now, depending on where the remaining ball is positioned, it's your call to send him to your right with (Go) **Out!/Come Bye!** or to your left with (Go) **Out!/Away to Me!** When he is lined up perpendicular to the last ball, click to confirm he is correct and cue him with **Drive!** until the ball reaches you at the goal line.

Step 11: When the last ball comes to you at the goal line, reward your dog *generously* and then cue him to lie **Down**. Say "**That'll Do!**" immediately to release your dog and step away from the goal line.

Repeat until your dog has performed the behavior with 80% reliability, before increasing your criteria for distance or time.

Lesson 4

Now that your dog can move right and left on cue at distance and stand directly behind the ball you've chosen, you increase the number of balls your dog will drive to you while maintaining his concentration and ball control.

Exercise 1: Your dog will start from the starting target at 10 o'clock, will (Go) Out!, Come Bye! and Line-up behind a line of three balls without a point target. Moving left, right or center, the dog will drive those balls one at a time to you at the goal.

This is a positioning exercise for better control, and for that reason we lower our criterion: the distance to the goal. Place three balls (the same or different sizes) in a straight, horizontal line, six to ten feet from the goal line. Place the starting target at the 10 o'clock position, but do not place a target behind the line of balls. Your dog will be sent from the start target to **Come Bye!** and then be cued to move left, right or center, to stand behind the ball you wish him to bring. He will be rewarded for lining up correctly and then be cued to **Drive!** the ball to you.

Step 1: Step off on your left foot and use your loose leash walking cue (**Heel** or **Let's go**) to walk your dog out to the starting target.

Step 2: When you reach the starting target, place your dog in a **Down**. Click on the **Down** and toss a treat onto the ground near the target.

Step 3: Add your verbal and hand signal cue to **Stay** and return to your starting position in front of the goal.

Step 4: Step off on your right foot and using your right hand, or the target stick held in your right hand, turn to face your dog and cue him to move with (Go) **Out!/Come Bye.**

Step 5: Click the dog when he moves to stand behind the row of balls, then toss a treat out behind the balls.

Step 6: Align *your* position in the goal area to each ball in turn, cueing him with (Go) **Come Bye!** or (Go) **Away to Me!** to move him right or left, and **Line-up** for positioning him correctly behind each ball. On each straight placement, click and toss a treat out behind the balls.

Step 7: After moving him right, left or center and treating each time, choose a specific ball. Align your position in the goal area to that ball and simply wait for him to align his position to *you*.

Step 8: When he is lined up perpendicular to the ball you've chosen, click again to confirm he is in the correct place and then cue him to **Drive!** until the ball reaches you at the goal. Click and reward him immediately before sending him out again.

Step 9: Now choose one of the remaining balls and send him out in the appropriate direction. Cue him with (Go) **Out!/Come Bye!** or (Go) **Out!/Away to Me!** to move him right or left depending on which ball you wish him to bring and click when he stands behind the chosen ball.

Step 10: Cue him with **Drive!** until that ball reaches you at the goal. Click and reward him immediately before sending him out again.

Step 11: Now send him back out, left with (Go) **Out!/Come Bye!** or right with (Go) **Away to Me!** to bring the last ball to the goal. When he is lined up perpendicular to the ball you've chosen, click again to confirm he is in the correct place, and then cue him with **Drive!** until the ball reaches you at the goal.

Step 12: When the last ball is in the goal, cue him to lie **Down** and reward him generously. Say **"That'll Do!"** to release him and take a few steps away from the goal.

Repeat until your dog has performed the behavior with 80% reliability, before increasing your criteria for distance or time. Build up to 80% reliability in five foot increments, moving from 15 to 25 feet.

Exercise 2: Your dog will move from the Start position with (Go) Out!/Come Bye!, and respond to successive cues: Watch me!, Stand, Drive! and Down, and then move three to five balls to you from fifteen feet to the goal before being released with That'll Do! at the goal line

Set for Come Bye! Three balls and Start target on the left.

Set for Come Bye! Five balls and Start target on the left.

Place three to five balls in the field, fifteen feet out from the goal in a triangle formation with the point ball placed farthest from the goal. If you choose to work with three balls, place them in a triangle formation with the point ball behind the two balls in front. If you choose to work with five balls, place three in front and two behind them, one slightly offset, which will be designated as the point ball. Place one flat target behind the point ball (at 12 o'clock) and place the small target at your left (at 10 o'clock) of the ball-set.

You (the handler) do not move into the field.

Step 1: With your dog on your left side, step out on your left foot and use your walking cue (**Heel** or **Let's go**) to take your dog out to the starting target, at 10 o'clock. When you reach the starting target, place your dog in a **Down**. Click on the **Down** and toss a treat onto the ground near the target.

Step 2: Now add your verbal and hand signal cues for **Stay** and return to your starting position at the goal line.

Step 3: Turn to face your dog, then step out on your right foot and use your right hand, or the target stick in your right hand, to signal him to move to your right. Say "**<Your dog's name>**, (Go) **Out!/Come Bye!**" to send him to the far target.

Step 4: Click as he moves (to his left) to the far target.

Step 5: Now use your upright hand signal and say "**Watch me!**" to have him focus on you for the next cue. Click when his eyes make contact with yours.

Lesson #4
Exercise #2

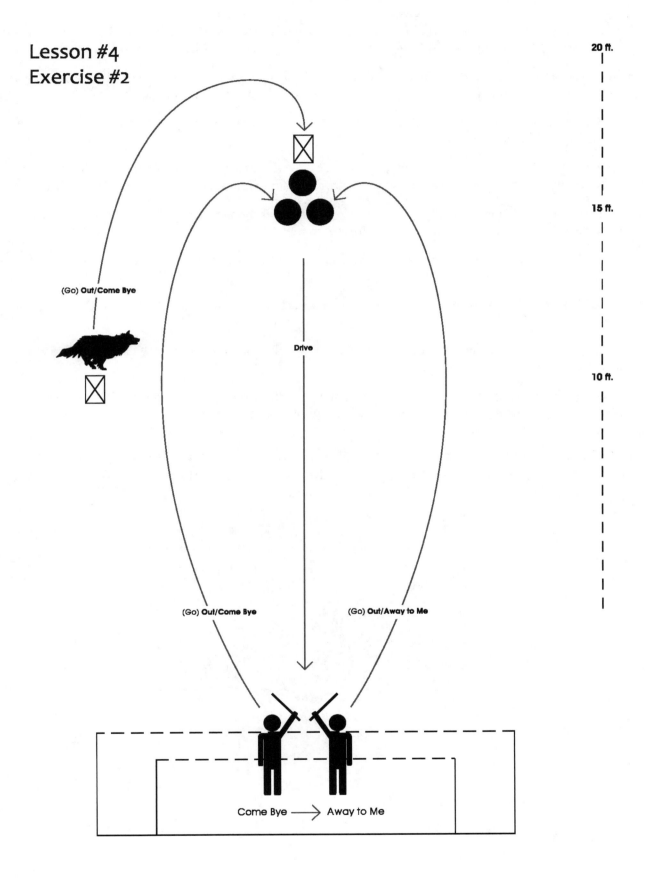

20 ft.

15 ft.

10 ft.

(Go) **Out/Come Bye**

Drive

(Go) **Out/Come Bye**

(Go) **Out/Away to Me**

Come Bye ⟶ Away to Me

Step 6: Cue your dog to **Stand** on the target and click when he is lined up behind the point ball perpendicular to you. Use the Line-up, **Back** or **Walk-on!** cues, if necessary, to put him in the most correct position.

Step 7: Say "**<Your dog's name>, Drive!**" and click on the forward motion of the ball until it reaches you at the goal line. Reward him immediately before sending him out to gather the remaining balls.

Step 8: Step out on your left foot and use your left hand, or the target stick in your left hand, to send the dog out to his right behind the balls with **"Away to Me!"**

Step 9: Click to confirm when he lines up perpendicular to your choice of the remaining balls. Now, cue him to **"Drive!"** until that ball reaches you at the goal line. Reward him immediately before sending him out again.

Step 10: Depending on where the last ball is positioned, you will choose to send him to your right with (Go) **Out!/Come Bye!** or to your left with (Go) **Out!/Away to Me!**

Step 11: When he arrives behind the ball, use the **Line-up, Back** or **Walk-on!** cues if necessary, to put him in the most correct position.

Step 12: When he lines up perpendicular to the last ball, cue him with **Drive!** until the ball reaches you at the goal line.

Step 13: Cue him to lie **Down** at the goal line. Give him a *BIG* reward (jackpot!) Say **"That'll Do!"** to release him and step away from the goal.

Repeat until he has reached 80% reliability in moving three balls correctly before adding more balls. Then get 80% reliability in moving five balls before increasing your practice distance.

Exercise 3: Your dog will start from your right side and move to your left with (Go) Out!/Away to Me!, then respond to all combining cues to drive three to five balls to you at the goal from a distance of ten to fifteen feet

Set for Away to Me! Three balls and Start target on the right.

Set for Away to Me! Five balls and Start target on the right.

Place three to five balls in the field, ten to fifteen feet out from the goal, in a triangle formation with the point ball placed farthest from the goal. If you choose to work with three balls, place them in a triangle formation with the point ball behind the two balls in front. If you choose to work with five balls, place three in front and two behind them, one slightly offset, which will be designated as the point ball. Place one flat target behind the point ball (at 12 o'clock) and place the other target at your right (at 2 o'clock) of the ball-set.

You (the handler) do not move into the field.

Step 1: With your dog on your left side, step out on your left foot and use your walking cue (**Heel** or **Let's go**) to take your dog out to the starting target, now placed to the right side of the ball-set, at 2 o'clock. When you reach the starting target, place your dog in a **Stand**. Click on the **Stand** and toss a treat onto the ground, near the target.

Step 2: Now add your hand and verbal signals to cue **Stand** and then return to your starting position at the goal.

Step 3: Turn to face your dog, step out on your left foot and use your left hand, or the target stick in your left hand, to signal him to move to your left (his right). Say **"<Your dog's name>, (Go) Out!/Away to Me!"** to send him to the far target.

Step 4: Click as the dog moves (to his right) to the far target behind the point ball.

Step 5: Now use your upright hand signal and say **"Watch me!"** to have him focus on you for the next cue. Click when his eyes make contact with yours.

Step 6: Cue your dog to **Stand** on the target and click when he is lined up perpendicular to you. If he overshoots the ball, use the **Back** cue. If he needs to move forward, use **Walk-on!** to have him move up slowly.

Step 7: Say **"<Your dog's name>, Drive!"** and click on the forward motion of the ball until the point ball reaches you at the goal line. Reward him immediately before sending him out to gather the remaining balls.

Step 8: Depending on your choice of the next ball, send him to your right with (Go) **Out!/Come Bye!** or to your left with (Go) **Out!/Away to Me!**

Step 9: When he lines up perpendicular to you behind the ball you have chosen, click to confirm before cueing him to **"Drive!"** When the ball reaches you at the goal line, reward him immediately before sending him out again.

Step 10: Depending on where the last ball is positioned, you will choose to send him to your right with (Go) **Out!/Come Bye!** or to your left with (Go) **Out!/Away to Me!**

Lesson #4
Exercise #3

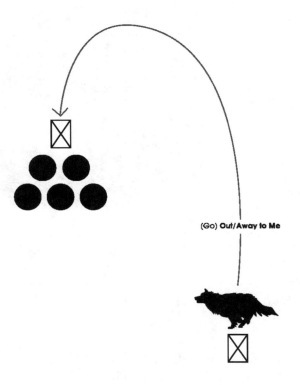

(Go) **Out/Away to Me**

20 ft.

15 ft.

10 ft.

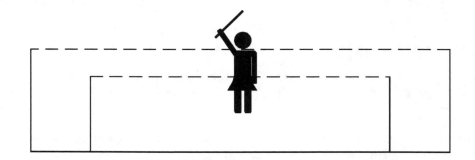

Step 11: If he overshoots the ball, use the **Back** cue. If he needs to move forward, use **Walk-on!** to have him move up slowly.

Step 12: When he lines up perpendicular to you behind the last ball, cue him with **Drive!** until the ball reaches you at the goal line.

Step 13: Cue him to lie **Down** at the goal line. Give him a *BIG* reward (jackpot!) Say **"That'll Do!"** to release him and step away from the goal.

Repeat five times or until he has reached 80% reliability in moving three balls correctly before adding more balls. Then get 80% reliability in moving five balls before increasing your practice distance.

Lesson 5

Now that you have worked on positioning and control, you will raise your criteria to increase the distance in the field and the number of balls your dog will drive to you to the full set of eight. In Exercise 2, the ground targets are no longer necessary since your dog is moving and positioning himself accurately via your directional cues. At this point in your training, begin using all directional cues independently of each other, to place him in the most advantageous field position.

Exercise 1: Your dog will move from a Down in the starting position (at 10 o'clock), then (Go) Out! and Come Bye! When he reaches the position behind the point ball, he will orient to you with Watch me!, Stand on cue and wait for release with That'll Do!

Fin lines up behind a full ball-set.

Place five balls in the field at twenty feet out from the goal line, in a triangle formation, with the point ball farthest from the goal (at 12 o'clock).

You (the handler) do not move into the field.

Step 1: With your dog on your left side, step out on your left foot and use your walking cue (**Heel** or **Let's go**) to take your dog out to the starting position (at 10 o'clock.) When you reach the position, place your dog in a **Down**.

Step 2: Now add the verbal and hand signal cues for **Stay** and return to your starting position at the goal.

Step 3: When you reach the goal, turn and face him. Step out on your right foot and use your right hand, or the target stick in your right hand, to cue him to (Go) **Out!/Come Bye!,** or simply say **"<Your dog's name>, Come Bye!"** Click as he moves around the balls and comes to the 12 o'clock position behind the point ball.

Step 4: Say **"Watch me!"** for attention and click when he makes eye contact.

Step 5: Cue him to **Stand** on the target. Walk up to him and reward him by tossing a treat onto the ground near the target. Say **"That'll Do!"** to release him and take a few steps away.

Repeat until your dog has performed the behavior with 80% reliability before increasing the criteria for distance.

Exercise #2: Your dog will move from the Start position, (Go) Out! and right with Come Bye! When he reaches the starting position behind the point ball, he will orient to you with Watch me! and drive five to eight balls to the goal, changing direction on cue and waiting for release with That'll Do!

Kita Downs at the 10 o'clock position with all targets removed.

You (the handler) do not move into the field.

Place five to eight balls in a triangle formation, twenty feet from the goal, with the point ball at 12 o'clock. Your dog will move all of the balls to you at the goal.

Step 1: With your dog on your left side, step out on your left foot and use your walking cue (**Heel** or **Let's go**) to take your dog out to the **Start** position at 10 o'clock. When you reach the position, place your dog in a **Down**, add the verbal and hand signal cues for **Stay** and then return to your starting position at the goal.

Step 2: Say **"Watch me!"** to cue your dog to focus on your face before giving the next cue. Click when he makes eye contact.

At this point in a Treibball match, the timekeeper would give you the signal to start your run.

Step 3: When you reach the goal, turn and face him. Step out on your right foot and use your right hand, or the target stick in your right hand, to cue him to (Go) **Out!/Come Bye!**, or simply say **"<Your dog's name>, Come Bye!"** Click as he moves around the balls and comes to the 12 o'clock position behind the point ball.

Step 4: Cue your dog to Stand, and use any other necessary directionals (**Line-up, Back, Out!** or **Walk-on!**) to ensure he is lined up directly perpendicular to the point ball.

Step 5: Say **"Drive!"** until the point ball comes to you at the goal and reward him before sending him back out to gather the next ball.

Step 6: Now choose a second ball, to your left, to be brought in. Step out on your left foot and use your left hand, or your target stick in your left hand, to send him around the remaining balls with **Away to Me!**

Step 7: Click on the correct movement, as he comes around the balls.

Step 8: Cue him to **Stand** again when he is squarely behind the second ball you want him to bring in. Use any other necessary directionals (**Line-up, Back, Out!** or **Walk-on!**) to ensure he is lined up directly perpendicular to the ball.

Step 9: Cue **Drive!** until the second ball comes to the goal. Reward him at the goal line with a tossed treat.

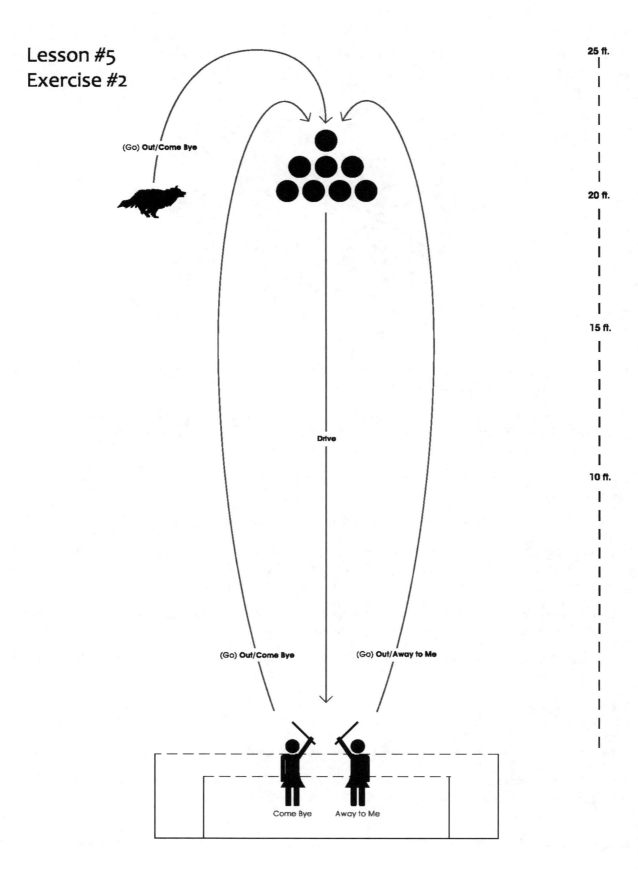

Lesson #5
Exercise #2

(Go) Out/Come Bye

Drive

(Go) Out/Come Bye

(Go) Out/Away to Me

Come Bye

Away to Me

25 ft.

20 ft.

15 ft.

10 ft.

Step 10: Now choose a third ball to your right to be brought in. Use your right hand, or the target stick in your right hand, to cue him to (Go) **Out!/Come Bye!**, or simply say **"<Your dog's name>, Come Bye!"** Click as he moves around the remaining balls and comes to stand behind the ball you have chosen.

Step 11: Cue him with **Watch me!** if you need to regain his attention, or simply cue him to Stand when he is squarely behind the third ball you want him to bring in, or use any necessary directionals (**Line-up, Back, Out!** or **Walk-on**!) to insure he is lined up directly behind that ball.

Step 12: Align your body position directly with his and when you are standing on opposite sides of the ball from each other, cue him to **Drive!** until that ball comes to the goal. Reward him at the goal line, with a tossed treat.

Step 13: Depending on your choice of those balls, you will repeat the process, using all your directional cues to achieve the most correct positioning to drive those remaining balls to the goal.

Step 14: When the final ball comes to the goal, cue your dog to lie **Down** and offer him a *BIG* reward (jackpot!).

At this point the Timekeeper or judge would signal the end of your run.

Step 15: Say **"That'll Do!"** to release him and take a few steps away.

Repeat until he has reached 80% reliability in moving five balls correctly before increasing the number to the full ball-set of eight. Repeat until he has reached 80% reliability in moving eight balls before increasing your practice distance to more than twenty feet.

Lesson 6

This lesson involves setting up a practice game with a full set of eight balls using official distance and timing.

As we come to the end of the Intermediate training lesson plan you and your dog should be comfortable moving the entire ball-set to the goal area anywhere from 20 feet out to the full distance of 37.5 feet. If you are not, that simply means you need a bit more practice. So, simply step back and break the lessons down further into more manageable segments. Remember, this is supposed to be fun for you both! When you feel confident enough to do so, set up a practice run, using actual timing and distance. You may click to confirm each correct movement, but can only offer the reward at the end of the run. Keep your voice light and animated as you give your dog the cues. Now's the time to get in the spirit of the game and have fun!

Full set of eight balls, placed midfield with the point farthest from the goal.

Place all eight balls mid-field, in a triangle, with the point/peak ball placed farthest from the goal. For example, for a Standard size dog (measuring 17.1 inches and over at the shoulder), in a 75 foot long area, the front line of four balls would be placed at the 37.5 foot mark. For a Toy breed/Small size dog (measuring 17 inches and under at the shoulder), in a 40 foot field, the front line of balls would be placed at the 20 foot mark.

Your spacing for ball placement will vary slightly, based on the size of the balls you're using. Remember, the balls can be of differing sizes or all of the same size, as long as they are physically appropriate to the size of your dog. Set the back of your goal at the zero-foot mark, with a four foot area marked around it. An actual goal area, marked with tape, chalk or other demarcation may be used to give you a visual of where to stand and what constitutes a score. The standard size of a physical goal is a minimum of five feet deep and twelve to fourteen feet long.

Set your goal line at the zero foot mark. The goal you're using should be deep enough to hold all eight balls, with enough room for you to stand inside and to move within the boundaries. An actual goal line of tape, chalk or other demarcation may be used to indicate this area in front of the actual goal. The standard goal size is a minimum of five feet deep by twelve to fourteen feet long.

Use a stopwatch, an oven timer, or enlist the aid of a friend to be your timekeeper. Set your timer for ten minutes and have your timekeeper ready to signal you to start.

Walk your dog out to the **Start** position and ask him to lie **Down**. For a Standard size dog in a 75 foot long area, the Start position is defined as being 33 feet from back of the goal and 9 feet in from the side of the field. For a Toy breed/Small size dog in a 40 foot field, the Start position is defined as being 16 feet from the back of the goal, and 7 feet in from the side of the field.

Walk back to the goal area and stand at the front or in the center of the goal. Turn to face your dog and use your upright hand signal for **Watch me!** to keep him focused on you until you get the start signal.

Signal your Timekeeper to set the timer for ten minutes, and give you a 'Start' signal.

When your timekeeper says **"Start,"** say **"<Your dog's name> Out!** and **Come Bye!"** to send him clockwise around the ball-set. Cue him to **Stand** when he lines up behind the point ball. Use any of your directional cues or **Line up**, to position him properly behind the ball-set.

Chance Stands behind the ball-set and Watches.

Cue him to **Drive!** the point ball to you. Praise him when he brings it to the goal, and send him back out to get the second ball.

Praise your dog when he drives the ball to the goal.

As the ball-set breaks up, use your directional cues to send him left or right depending on which way the next chosen ball lies. Use any of your directional cues to send him in the correct direction, line him up properly behind each choice and then to keep going!

Eloise responds to the Back signal to reposition behind the correct ball.

Cue him to **Drive!** each ball to you. As each ball comes to the goal, praise your dog before sending him out with new directions to bring in the next ball.

Sakara lies Down at the goal when all the balls are in.

When all the balls are in the goal, or when your timekeeper calls time, cue your dog to lie **Down** at the goal line and offer him a BIG reward (jackpot), before releasing him by saying **"That'll Do!"** Then tell him he's wonderful!!

Now you're playing Treibball!

5

Advanced Treibball Training

The Advanced section provides more difficult enhancements to the game. Those enhancements require you and your dog to use real problem-solving skills, in real time, as you might when working outdoors as a team and encountering challenges such as obstacles or erratically moving livestock. Diagrams have been added later in this section to help illustrate the more complex exercises.

Now that your dog can reliably move all eight balls to the goal in the required time frame and at the proper distance, it's time to add some enhancements that build even better teamwork through increasing your dog's problem-solving skills. Advanced Treibball presents both physical and mental challenges your dog may not have encountered before.

If you think of the eight Treibball balls like the sheep or livestock they represent, you will understand that those living "*herdables*" might move in an uneven manner. They might wander downhill or end up behind obstacles (like rocks, sheds or bushes), or they might need to be brought in a specific order, not known by the handler, until the time occurs.

So, in the lessons that follow, we will concentrate on more precise ball herding and handler positioning. The following exercises introduce the challenge of herding the balls in a lateral motion, moving the balls around one or more obstacles, numbering or sorting the balls in a specific order and adding odd-shaped balls that might move in an irregular manner. Each of these challenges for you and your dog will require more directional control. Since your dog will need more direction from you to adapt to these changing environments, you will need to adjust your physical position in relation to that of your dog so that the balls come directly to you in the goal within the required time frame.

In Advanced level play, additional challenges may be given to the handler, administered by the goal line judge. These include:

Numbering challenges
Decals or marker can be used to number the balls in play. Since bringing in the point ball first with only one cue earns three bonus points or 45 seconds off your final time *the handler is always encouraged to have the dog bring whichever ball is at the point of the ball-set first, and then continue in a variety of ordering formats:*

- Judges may have pre-chosen numbering scenarios to give the handler.

- The handler may request to choose his ordering slip at random from a basket and direct his dog to bring the balls in that order.

- A judge may choose the ordering slip at random from the basket and give it to the handler.

- Balls can be brought in random numbering order. For example: 2-5-1-8-4-6-7-3.

- Judges can direct that all even numbered balls come to the goal first, and then the odd numbered balls: 2-4-6-8, then 1-3-5-7.

- Reverse order next, odd numbered balls first, then the even numbered balls: 1-3-5-7 then 2-4-6-8.

Ordering challenges, the judge calls by size, for example:

- All the large balls are brought in first, then the smaller balls.

- All the smaller balls are brought in first, then the larger balls.

- One large, then one small, alternating between the sizes.

- Reverse order next, one small, then one large.

Or the judge can call by color or shape:

- All balls of one color first. For example, all red balls of any size, and then all remaining balls of any color.

- All red balls, and then all blue balls, then green balls, etc.

- All light-colored balls before the dark-colored balls. For example: pink, white, yellow, before red, black, dark blue and silver.

- Reverse order next, the dark-colored balls before the light-colored balls. For example: blue, black, silver and dark green, before pink, white and yellow.

- Judge may call the colors to the handler, individually. For example: red, black, white, blue, green, silver, pink and yellow.

- Oddly shaped balls may be added, up to three per ball-set. Judge may call out the colors or shapes to the handler.

The judge may ask that your dog bring the balls in order by size, color or even shape.

For Excellent and Champion level play, obstacles and barriers are introduced to simulate the dog gathering sheep that may have wandered. Dependent on the level of play, a maximum of four obstacles may be selected with the remainder of the balls, regulation-sized or odd-shaped, in the field in classic formation. *As before, the ball that is set at the point will be the one the dog is directed to gather first.* Obstacles may include: large potted plants or trees, hay bales, chairs, a folding screen, a small landscaping bridge, one or more traffic cones or draped barriers of differing sizes and lengths.

As you advance, you move from only using regulation-size balls (25 cm to 45 cm) for Toy breed/Small size dogs, and (45-75 cm) for Standard size dogs, to adding some oddly or irregular-shaped balls, and finally some simple barriers and obstacles that your dog must work around. As he becomes more accomplished at adapting to these challenges, more obstacles and problem-solving challenges can be added.

Treibball is a game that can grow with you and your dog. It is a thinking game that increases your ability to work as a team whatever challenges may occur.

In this section all the exercises are shown, by picture or diagram, at full-field distance. For your practice purposes, work at half or even a third of regulation distance (relative to the size of your dog) until your dog has mastered the exercise, then move your field of play back in increasingly increments until you achieve the full-field distances required for Teacup or Standard regulation play. Also, as you work through this section where the tasks are harder to perform, remember to mark and reward every correct execution of the performed behavior.

As your dog becomes more accomplished, you will raise your criteria to reward him only on the completion of the movement or task, or to reward him for the best execution of that task. As you vary his rate of reward, begin to substitute any of the verbal markers your dog knows, such as **"Wait"** or **"Watch me"** as your **"Keep going"** signal and fade the use of the click.

The lessons and exercises included in this section are as follows:

- **Lesson 1**
  - Moving balls to the goal in order, adding odd-shaped irregular balls.
  - Aligning your body position to that of your dog.

- **Lesson 2**
  - Ground exercises for greater ball control.
  - Creating more fluid body movement.

- **Lesson 3**
  - Ground exercises for training lateral movement.

- **Lesson 4**
  - Using the **(Go) Out!** cue with ground targets and ground obstacles within the field.
  - Dog will **(Go) Out!** to **Come Bye!** and/or **Away to Me!** to move behind an obstacle at a distance and drive one ball to the goal.

- **Lesson 5**
  - Introducing a larger obstacle to encourage your dog's problem-solving skills.
  - Refining your position at the goal.

- **Lesson 6**
  - Introducing a second barrier down-field. Dog will **(Go) Out!**, respond to **Come Bye!** and/or **Away to Me!** to move behind both obstacles.
  - At a distance, dog positions himself correctly to each ball's position and drives two balls to the goal.

- **Lesson 7**
  - Putting it all together with full-field exercises using multiple obstacles and regular and oddly-shaped/irregular balls that will be brought to the goal in order.

- **Lesson 8**
  - Problem solving scenarios: fine tuning your own approach to challenges in the field.

Lesson 1

In this lesson, the concept of moving the balls to the goal in a specific order is introduced. Balls can be moved to the handler at the goal by size number or by color, according to the handler or judge's direction. These exercises are similar to Lesson 5 of the Intermediate level, with the emphasis on your body position in relation to the center line of your dog and the ball, and then adding a specified ordering of the balls to be brought to the goal.

Just as a soccer goalie adjusts his position within the goal to the direction of the ball, you will move along with your dog, creating a fluid motion. When your spine lines up directly toward your dog, a direct center line is created between you which results in greater accuracy in driving the ball to you. It allows your dog to bring the balls in a correct trajectory to you, at whatever position you choose in the goal.

In American Treibball Association scoring, bringing the point ball in with as few cues as possible results in Bonus points of 15-45 seconds being subtracted from your final time. So, for our training purposes, the ball that is placed at the point position will be designated #1, be brought in first and driven directly to the goal, regardless of shape, size or color.

Exercise 1: You will begin in the center of the goal giving directional cues using your hand signals, target stick or voice, and adjusting your position to the alignment of your dog

Begin at the full distance to the goal, with the point ball placed 37.5 feet from the goal for Standard size dogs, or at 20 feet from the goal for Toy breed/small dogs. Five balls are placed in the triangle formation, with the point ball farthest from the goal.

Chance stands behind the point ball.

Step 1: With your dog in a **Down** at the **Start** position, at 10 o'clock, stand in the center of the goal. Turn slightly to your left so that your spine is aligned with the spine of your dog.

Step 2: Step out on your right foot and use your right hand, or the target stick in your right hand, to cue him to move out to your right. Say **"<Your dog's name>, Come Bye!"** and move to your right toward the center of the goal.

Step 3: Click as your dog moves into the correct position behind the point ball. Give him the cue to **Drive!** If the ball does not roll in a direct line to you, use your directional cues, (Go) **Out!/Come Bye!** or (Go) **Out!/ Away to Me!** to further align your dog with your position so that the ball comes directly to you. Your spine should always be aligned with your dog's spine and the midpoint of the ball.

If the ball does not roll in a direct line to you, use your directional cues (Go)**Out!/Come Bye, Back, Line-up** or (Go)**Out!/Away to Me!** as necessary, to better align your dog with your position in the goal. Your spine should always be aligned with your dog's spine and the midpoint of the ball.

Step 4: Next the dog will bring the ball in the #2 position, second from the right in the front line, leaving balls #3 through #5 in place. Use your judgment as to which cue will cause your dog to bring the ball to you at the goal in the most efficient manner.

If you want to send him out and around to your left, step out on your left foot and use your left hand, or the target stick in your left hand, to cue him to move him into position, again using (Go) **Out!/Away to Me!**

If you think a straight path up the middle of the set would be easier or faster, step out on your right foot, and use your right hand, or the target stick in your right hand, to cue him to move into position, using (Go) **Out!/ Come Bye.**

Step 5: Since he is moving to the middle of the ball-set, you may need to further refine his position, using the **Back** and **Line-up** cues, to position him squarely behind the #2 ball. As he lines up in the correct position behind the ball, align your body position to match your dog's alignment. Click to confirm before adding the cue to **Drive!** When that ball comes to you at the goal, praise him and reward him by tossing a treat out before sending him out to get the next ball.

Step 6: Since #3 is in the center-left position, move to the center-right of the goal area and choose either (Go) **Out!/Come Bye!** or (Go) **Out!/Away to Me!** to move him around the outer balls (#5 and #4) to position him squarely behind the #3 ball.

Step 7: Adjust your position to meet your dog's spinal alignment, moving left or right, within the goal area. As he lines up in the correct position, click and add the cue to **Drive!** When that ball comes to you at the goal, reward him by tossing a treat out before sending him out to get the next ball.

Step 8: Since ball #4 will be to your far right, move slightly to your left, step out on your right foot and use your right hand, or the target stick in your right hand, to cue him to move to your right, with **Come Bye!** Now your dog and ball #4 have a clear center path to you at the goal.

Step 9: Click as he lines up in the correct position behind the ball and add the cue to **Drive!** Based on the position of the ball, align your body position to meet that of your dog, moving left or right within the goal area. When that ball comes to the goal, reward him by tossing a treat out before sending him out to get the next ball.

Step 10: Ball #5 remains, on your left, so the final cue will be a (Go) **Out!/Away to Me!** to bring the last ball to the goal. Step out on your left foot and use your left hand, or the target stick in your left hand, to move him out and to your left. Say **"<Your dog's name>, (Go) Out!/Away to Me!"** and move to your right to stand in the center of the goal. Now your dog and ball #5 have a clear center path to you at the goal. Click as he lines up in the correct position behind the last ball, align yourself with your dog's position and add the cue to **Drive!**

Step 11: When the final ball comes to you at the goal, cue your dog to **Down** and reward him with a *jackpot*! Release your dog by saying **"That'll Do!"** and take a few steps away.

Only when your dog is reliably moving all five balls to you in order, *adapting his position to yours in the goal area* in 80% of his attempts do you raise your criteria and require a greater number of balls be brought to the goal before varying or changing your rate of reward. In addition, only when all five balls are being moved to the goal in a complete, fluid motion, in 80% of attempts, do you raise your criteria to add more balls (up to the full complement of 8 balls) *or* replace one ball with an oddly-shaped, irregular ball.

Exercise 2: You will begin in the left-center of the goal, give directional cues, using your hand signals, target stick or voice, adjusting your position to the alignment of your dog

Begin again at the full distance from the goal, placing five balls in a triangle position with the point ball farthest from the goal and with the first odd-shaped or irregular ball on the outside corner in the #4 position. Oddly-shaped, irregular balls are weighted differently and will move more erratically than standard balls, so more minute adjustments in the alignment between you and your dog will be necessary to move them to the goal efficiently.

Chance will Come Bye and go Away to Me to Drive all balls, in order, to the goal.

Step 1: With your dog in a **Down** at the **Start** position, at 10 o'clock, stand in the center of the goal area. Turn slightly to your left so that your spine is aligned with the spine of your dog.

Step 2: Step out on your right foot and use your right hand, or the target stick in your right hand, to cue him to move out and to your right. Say **"<Your dog's name>, (Go) Out!/Come Bye!"** and move to your right to stand in the center of the goal. Click as your dog moves into the correct position behind the point ball. Align your body position to that of your dog.

Step 3: If the ball does not roll in a direct line to you, use your directional cues (Go) **Out!/Come Bye, Back, Line-up** or (Go) **Out!/Away to Me!** as necessary, to better align your dog with your position in the goal. Your spine should be aligned with your dog's spine and the midpoint of the ball.

If the ball rolls to the right, you will move to your left within the goal area and cue your dog to **Drive!** again. If the ball moves left, you will move to your right. Click as the ball in the point position comes to you at the goal. Praise your dog and toss a treat out before sending him to get the next ball.

Step 4: Next the dog will bring in the ball from the #2 position, second from the right in the front line, leaving balls #3 through #5 in place. Step out on your left foot and use your left hand, or the target stick in your left hand, to cue him to move him into position, again using **"<Your dog's name>, Away to Me!"**

Step 5: Since your dog is moving to the middle of the ball-set, you may need to further refine his position, using the **Back, Walk-on, Line-up,** (Go) **Out!/Come Bye!** or (Go) **Out!/Away to Me!** cues to position him squarely behind the #2 ball. As he lines up in the correct position, adjust your position to meet his alignment, moving left or right, within the goal area. Click to confirm before adding the cue to **Drive!**

Step 6: When that ball comes to you at the goal, praise him and reward him by tossing a treat out before sending him out to get the next ball.

Step 7: Since #3 is in the center-left position, move to the center-right of the goal area and choose either (Go) **Out!/Come Bye!** or (Go) **Out!/Away to Me!** to move him around the outer balls (#5 and #4) to position him squarely behind the #3 ball. Adjust your position to meet your dog's spinal alignment, moving left or right, within the goal area. As he lines up in the correct position, click and add the cue to Drive! When that ball comes to you at the goal, reward him by tossing a treat out before sending him out to get the next ball.

Step 8: Since the oddly-shaped, irregular ball is in the #4 position to your right, move slightly to your left within the goal, step out on your right foot and use your right hand, or the target stick in your right hand, to cue your dog to move right with (Go) **Out!/Come Bye**.

It will be your decision how to direct your dog to **Drive!** that ball from either side. If the ball is elliptical and therefore weighted on one end, you will change your own body alignment in the goal to match the weighted end of the ball and give the appropriate directional cue—(Go) **Out!/Come Bye!/Drive!**or (Go) **Out!/Away to Me!/Drive!**—to move the weighted end first.

If the oddly-shaped or irregular ball is elliptical or peanut-shaped, the ends may, or may not, be weighted equally (depending on the type or manufacturer of the ball.) Either way, these balls can be moved from the direct center most effectively.

Step 9: Once you have given the proper directional cue, click as the dog lines up in the correct position. Based on the position of the ball, adjust your position to meet your dog's alignment, moving left or right within the goal area.

Step 10: Depending on the erratic path of that ball, continue to align yourself with your dog as he moves from side to side and use your directional cues as often as needed—(Go) **Out!/Come Bye!/Drive!** or (Go) **Out!/Away to Me!/Drive!**—to direct your dog to the goal. When that ball comes to the goal, reward him by tossing a treat out before sending him out to get the next ball.

Step 11: Ball #5 remains on your left, so the final cue will be an **Away to Me!** to bring the last ball to the goal. Step out on your left foot and use your left hand, or the target stick in your left hand, to move him out and to your left. Say **"<Your dog's name>, (Go) Out!/Away to Me!"** and move to your right to stand in the center of the goal. Click as he lines up in the correct position behind the last ball, align yourself with your dog's position and add the cue to **Drive!**

Step 12: When the final ball comes to you at the goal, cue your dog to **Down** and reward him with a *jackpot*! Release your dog by saying **"That'll Do!"** and take a few steps away.

Only when your dog is reliably moving all five balls to you in order *while adapting his position to yours in the goal area* in 80% of his attempts, raise your criteria and require a greater number of balls be brought to the goal before varying or changing your rate of reward. In addition, only when your dog is reliably moving all five balls to you *in order*, with total control of the oddly-shaped, irregular ball while *adapting his body position to yours*, raise your criteria and require two or three balls to be moved to the goal before offering the dog a reward. Then vary the position of the irregular ball or add another odd-shaped ball to the ball-set.

Exercise 3: You will begin in the center of the goal, give directional cues using your hand signals, target stick or voice, adjusting your position to the alignment of your dog

Begin at full distance from the goal, placing all eight balls in a triangle position with the point ball farthest from the goal. Two of these are oddly-shaped, irregular balls.

Balls will be driven to the goal in order, including two irregular-shaped balls.

Step 1: With your dog in the **Start** position, at 10 o'clock, stand in the center of the goal area. Step out on your right foot and use your right hand, or the target stick in your right hand, to cue him to move to your right. Say **"<Your dog's name>, (Go) Out!/Come Bye!"**.

Step 2: Click as your dog moves to your right and click again when he is in the correct position behind the point ball. Give him the cue to **Drive!**

Adjust your position in the goal area accordingly and click as the ball in the point position comes to you at the goal. Praise your dog and toss a treat out before sending him to get the next ball.

Step 3: Next he will bring the ball in the #2 position, the first ball to your left in the second row, leaving balls #3 through #8 in place. Turn slightly to face ball #2 and say **"<Your dog's name>, (Go) Out!/Come Bye!"** to send him right again behind ball #2. Move to your right to stand in the right-center of the goal.

Step 4: As he lines up in the correct position, click to confirm and add the cue to **Drive!** Continue to adjust your position to meet that of your dog, moving left or right within the goal area. When that ball comes to the goal, praise him and reward him by tossing a treat out before sending him out to get the next ball.

Step 5: Since the oddly-shaped #3 ball is in the far right position of the second row, move to the center of the goal area and choose either (Go) **Out!/Come Bye!** to move him right outside and around the remaining balls, or (Go) **Out!/Away to Me!** to send him left up the inside to position him squarely behind the #3 ball.

Step 6: Once you have given the proper directional cue, click as your dog lines up in the correct position. Based on the position of the ball, adjust your position to meet his alignment, moving left or right within the goal area. Depending on the erratic path of that ball, continue to align yourself with your dog as he moves from side to side, and use your directional cues as often as needed—(Go) **Out!/Come Bye!/Drive!** or (Go) **Out!/Away to Me!/Drive!**)—to direct your dog to the goal.

Step 7: When that ball comes to the goal, reward him by tossing a treat out, before sending him out to get the next ball.

Step 8: Ball #4 is in the center position. Depending on the position of your dog, use either (Go) **Out!/Come Bye!** or (Go) **Out!/Away to Me!** to send him behind the #4 ball. Click as he lines up in the correct position and add the cue to **Drive!** When that ball comes to the goal, praise him and reward him by tossing a treat out before sending him to get the next ball.

Step 9: Now your dog must move left to gather the second oddly-shaped, irregular ball in the #5 position at the far left of the third row. Cue (Go) **Out!/Away to Me!** to send your dog behind the #5 ball and click as he lines up in the correct position. Add the cue to **Drive!**

Depending on the erratic path of that ball, continue to align yourself with your dog as he moves from side to side, and use your directional cues as often as needed—(Go) **Out!/Come Bye!/Drive!** or (Go) **Out!/Away to Me!/Drive!**—to direct your dog to the goal.

Step 10: When that ball comes to the goal, praise him and reward him by tossing a treat out before sending him to get the next ball.

Step 11: Ball #6 is left of center, so the next cue will be (Go) **Out!/Away to Me!** again to bring the ball to the goal. Click as he lines up in the correct position behind the ball, position yourself in the center right of the goal area and add the cue to **Drive!** When that ball comes to the goal, praise and reward him by tossing a treat out before sending him to get the next ball.

Step 12: Ball #7 is right of center in the second row, so the next cue will be a (Go) **Out!/Come Bye!** Click as he lines up in the correct position behind the ball, position yourself in the center left of the goal area and give your dog the cue to **Drive!** When that ball comes to the goal, praise him and reward him by tossing a treat out before sending him to get the next ball.

Step 13: Now only ball #8 remains, on the outside of the third row. Depending on the position of your dog, use either (Go) **Out!/Come Bye!** or (Go) **Out!/Away to Me!** to send him behind the #8 ball and click as he lines up in the correct position. Add the cue to **Drive!**

Step 14: When the final ball comes to you at the goal, cue your dog to lie **Down** and reward him with a *BIG* jackpot! Release him by saying **"That'll Do!"** and take a few steps away.

When your dog is reliably (80% of attempts) moving all eight balls to you *in order*, with total control of the irregular odd-shaped ball and *adapting his position to you in the goal area*, raise your criteria and require two or three balls to be moved to the goal before offering the dog a reward. Then vary the position of the irregular balls or introduce obstacles into the field of play.

Lesson 2

With this lesson we begin the development of more precise ball-handling skills. As your dog's skills become more accurate, a more fluid, lateral movement can be achieved in bringing in the balls to you at the goal. More fluid motion also allows your dog to make the needed adjustments in his body position, to orient himself and the ball to you from wherever it might roll.

Exercise 1: Figure 8 exercise for ball control

Using a field of 16 x 16 feet, place two traffic cones mid-field in a line ten feet apart at the 12 o'clock and 6 o'clock positions. Place one ball slightly to the right of the upper cone which is placed at 12 o'clock.

Begin with your dog in the **Start** position (at 10 o'clock). Cue your dog to **Come Bye!** to move around the upper cone and Drive! the ball to you *as you move backward* around the Figure 8. Your goal is to make a complete Figure 8, keeping the ball within a three-foot zone of both cones as you and your dog adjust your positions to each other. You will be clicking for placement and offering the reward at the end of the completed movement.

Winston makes a Figure 8 around the cones, keeping the ball within a three foot zone.

Lesson #2
Exercise #1

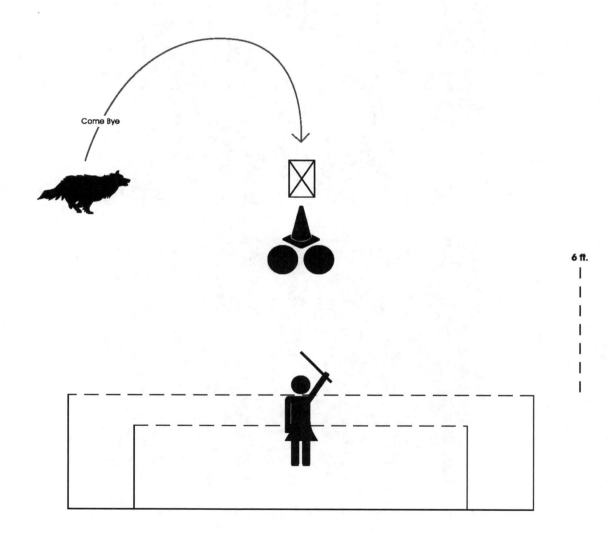

Come Bye

6 ft.

Step 1: With your dog in a **Down** in the **Start** position, stand three feet behind the upper cone, facing it. Step out on your right foot and use your right hand, or the target stick in your right hand, to cue him to move to your right. Say "**<Your dog's name>, Come Bye!**".

Step 2: Click as your dog moves around the cone to your right (his left) and click again as he comes behind the ball. When he is lined up perpendicular to you and the ball, cue him to **Drive!** and take a step back and to your left. As the ball moves toward you, click to confirm that's what you wanted and use the **Drive!** cue again if necessary.

Step 3: Back up and continue cueing your dog to **Drive!** *only if necessary.* If your dog will **Drive!** without cueing, simply click on each forward motion of the ball as long as the ball stays within that three foot zone directly in front of you. If the ball rolls outside of the three foot zone, stop and cue your dog with **Come Bye!, Away to Me!** or **Back** to move him into the correct position directly behind the ball.

Step 4: When you have made the complete Figure 8 and arrived back at the **Start** position, cue your dog to **Down** and reward him generously. Release him with **That'll Do!** and take a few steps away.

When your dog is moving reliably around the Figure 8 in a smooth fluid movement in 80% of his attempts, move each of the cones another four feet apart for a total distance of eighteen feet and repeat. When your dog is moving reliably around the Figure 8 with cones placed at eighteen feet apart in a smooth fluid movement in 80% of his attempts, move on to the next exercise.

Exercise 2: Now repeat the exercise, *with you standing in the center of the Figure 8*, only changing direction to face your dog as he moves the ball around the cones. You will cue your dog with hand/ target stick and voice signals only.

The goal is for your dog to make a complete Figure 8 around both cones, keeping the ball within three feet of each cone *as you remain stationary* and your dog adjusts his position to the ball and to you.

Winston makes a tight Figure 8 while the handler remains stationary.

Step 1: With your dog in the **Start** position, stand three feet behind the upper cone. Face the cone at 12 o'clock. Step out on your right foot and use your right hand, or the target stick in your right hand, to cue him to move to your right. Say "**<Your dog's name>, Come Bye!**"

Lesson #2
Exercise #2

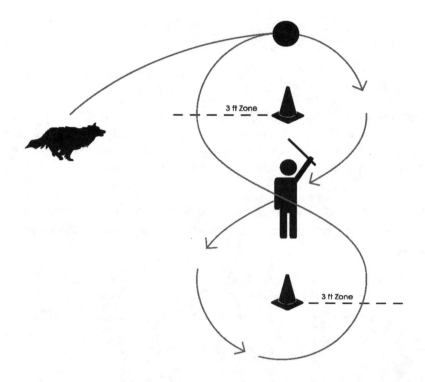

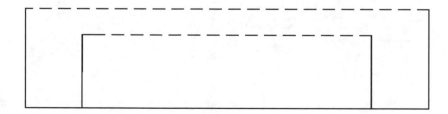

Dog begins in the **Start** position at 10 o'clock. Handler stands in the center of the figure 8 and turns to face the dog as he drives the ball around the cones, keeping the ball within a 3 ft. radius of each cone

Step 2: Click as your dog moves around the cone to your right (his left) and click again as he comes behind the ball. When he is lined up perpendicular to you and the ball, cue him to **Drive!** If your dog will **Drive!** without cueing, simply click on each forward motion of the ball as long as the ball stays within that three foot zone directly in front of you.

Step 3: As your dog comes towards you, at the midpoint of the Figure 8, transfer the target stick to your left hand or give the signal with your left hand, and then turn to face the 6 o'clock position and cue him with **Away to Me!/Drive!** to send him to your left (his right) around the lower cone. You may click on each forward motion of the ball if the ball stays within that three foot zone directly in front of you, or simply use the verbal cue to **Drive!** to encourage your dog to keep moving forward.

Step 4: If the ball rolls outside of the three foot zone, stop and cue your dog with **Come Bye, Away to Me, Line-up** or **Back**, to move him into the correct position directly behind the ball.

Step 5: When the dog approaches the midpoint again, turn to your right, transfer the stick to your right hand or use your right hand signal to cue him to **Come Bye!/Drive!**

Step 6: When your dog has made the complete Figure 8 and arrived back at the **Start** position, cue him to **Down** and reward him generously. Release your dog with **That'll Do!** and take a few steps away.

When your dog is moving reliably around the Figure 8 in a smooth fluid movement in 80% of his attempts, move each of the cones another four feet apart for a total distance of eighteen feet and repeat. When your dog is moving reliably around the Figure 8 with cones placed at eighteen feet apart in a smooth fluid movement in 80% of his attempts, move on to the next exercise.

Exercise 3: Double Figure 8

In this exercise, we add another cone in the center of the field, with the dog continuing to move the ball forward and keeping it within the three foot zone of each cone as he drives the ball to you.

Beginning with your dog in the **Start** position, you will cue your dog to **Come Bye!/Drive!** to move right around the upper cone and **Drive!** the ball to you *as you move backward left around the center cone then move right again around the lower cone.* Your goal is to make a Double Figure 8, keeping the ball within a three foot zone of all cones as you and your dog adjust your positions to each other.

Winston makes a tight Double Figure 8.

Lesson #2
Exercise #3

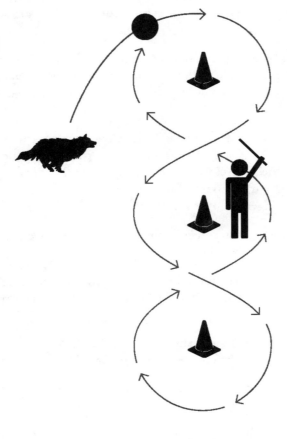

16 ft

8 ft

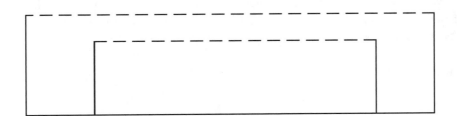

Dog begins in the **Start** position at 10 o'clock. Handler stands in the center and moves backward
or turns to face the dog, transferring the target stick to direct the dog left and right,
as the dog **Drives** the ball within a 3 ft. radius of each cone.

1 :: Regular balls first
2 :: Larger or odd/irregular-shaped ball next

Step 1: Stand three feet behind the uppermost cone, facing it. Step out on your right foot and use your right hand, or the target stick in your right hand, to cue him to move to your right. Say **"<Your dog's name>, Come Bye!"**

Step 2: Click as your dog moves around the first cone to your right (his left), and then click again as he comes behind the ball. When he is lined up perpendicular to the ball, cue him to **Drive!** and take a few steps back and to your left. As the ball moves toward you, click to confirm that what you wanted and use the **Drive!** cue again (*if necessary*).

Step 3: As your dog comes toward you at the center of the Double Figure 8, back up to the center cone and transfer the target stick to your left hand, or give the signal with your left hand, and turn to face the 6 o'clock position. Then cue him with **Away to Me!/Drive!** to send him to your left (his right) around the lower cone. Continue cueing your dog to **Drive!** only if necessary. If he will **Drive!** without cueing, simply click on each forward motion of the ball if the ball stays within that three foot zone directly in front of you.

If the ball rolls outside of the three foot zone, stop and cue your dog with **Come Bye!, Away to Me!** or **Back** or **Walk-on!** to move your dog into the correct position directly behind the ball.

Step 4: As he comes around the lower cone, use your right hand or transfer the target stick back to your right hand and cue **Come Bye!** to move him to your right around your position at the center cone before cueing him to **Drive!** again.

Step 5: Turn to face the upper cone and use your left hand signal, or transfer the target stick to your left hand and cue **Away to Me!** to move him to your left before cueing him to **Drive!** again.

Step 6: When your dog arrives back at the **Start** position, cue your dog to **Down** and reward him generously. Release him with **That'll Do!** and take a few steps away.

When your dog is moving reliably around the Double Figure 8 within that three foot zone in a smooth fluid movement in 80% of his attempts move each of the outer cones another four feet apart for a total distance of eighteen feet and repeat. When your dog is moving reliably around the Double Figure 8 with cones placed at eighteen feet apart in a smooth fluid movement in 80% of his attempts move on to the next exercise.

Exercise 4: Your dog will move from the Start position and Drive! the balls within three feet of each cone, now in a *horizontal*, fluid Figure 8

Using the same size field—16 square feet—turn the figure eight on its side, and take a position in the center of the goal area. Two traffic cones are placed mid-field in a line spaced ten feet apart, but now at the 9 o'clock and 3 o'clock positions. Place one ball above and slightly to the right of the 9 o'clock cone. You will stand in the center of the goal area and use your hand/target stick and voice signals only to send your dog to **Come Bye!** and **Away to Me!** by transferring the target stick from one hand to the other while you adjust your position in the goal area to your dog's body position in the field.

Winston Drives the ball around the 3 o'clock cone and heads for 9 o'clock before coming back to the center.

Step 1: With your dog in the **Start** position, step back to the center of the goal area. Face the cone at 3 o'clock. Step out on your right foot and use your right hand, or the target stick in your right hand, to cue him to move to your right. Say **"<Your dog's name>, Come Bye!"**

Step 2: Click as your dog moves around the upper cone to your right (his left) and click again as he comes behind the ball. When he is lined up perpendicular to the ball, cue him to **Drive!** As the ball moves toward the center, click to confirm that's what you wanted and use the **Drive!** cue again if necessary.

Step 3: As he comes toward the midpoint of the Figure 8, move to the center-right of the goal area and transfer the target stick to your left hand or give your dog the signal with your left hand. Cue him with **Away to Me!/ Drive!** to send him to your left (his right) around the 9 o'clock cone. You may click on each forward motion of the ball if the ball stays within that three foot zone, or simply use the verbal cue to **Drive!** to encourage your dog to keep moving forward.

Step 4: If the ball rolls outside of the three foot zone, stop and cue your dog with **Come Bye!, Away to Me!, Back** or **Walk-on!** to move your dog into the correct position directly behind the ball. As he comes around the left side of the Figure 8, add another **Drive!** cue and click on *any* forward motion of the ball.

This is the first instance in any of our lessons where the dog must **Drive!** the ball *away* from you. This is very difficult and goes against his prior training, so you will have to practice shaping this motion carefully.

Step 5: When your dog has made the complete Figure 8 and arrived back at the **Start** position, cue him to lie **Down** and reward him *very* generously. Release him with **That'll Do!** and take a few steps away.

When your dog is moving reliably around the Figure 8 in a smooth fluid movement in 80% of his attempts, move each of the cones another four feet apart for a total distance of eighteen feet and repeat. When your dog is moving reliably around the Figure 8 in a smooth fluid movement with cones placed at eighteen feet apart in 80% of his attempts, move on to the next exercise.

Lesson #2
Exercise #4

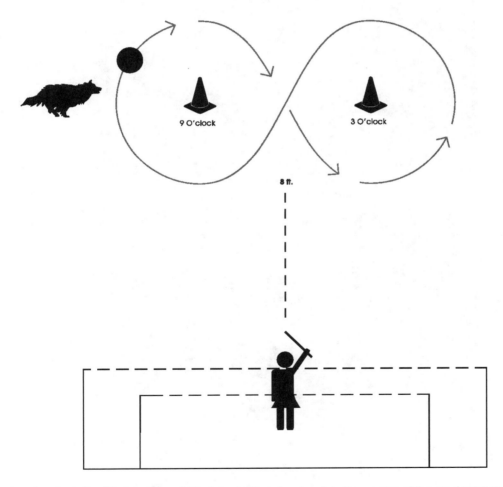

Dog begins in the **Start** position at 10 o'clock. Handler stands in the center of the goal area and transfers the target stick to direct the dog left and right, keeping the ball within a 3 ft. radius of each cone, placed at 9 and 3 o'clock.

Lesson 3

Now that you have sharpened your ball skills and become more aware of how your body alignment aids in directing your dog's movement of the balls (of any shape) to you at the goal, we will introduce some small obstacles and add distance exercises that incorporate all you've learned so far.

Exercise 1: Four Mat/Four Ball/Four Cone exercise to increase lateral control. Moving clockwise first, combining Come Bye!/Drive! to move each ball around the cone to you at the center.

We begin with a very short distance for control and accuracy. Using a field of 12 by 12 feet, place four mats six feet equidistant from the center of the field at 12, 3, 6, and 9 o'clock, with a ball in front of each mat and a traffic cone in front of each ball. You (the handler) will stand in the center of the square, direct your dog to each mat in turn and cue him to **Drive!** the ball to you.

Four mat/four ball/four cone set-up.

Fin Stands on the target and Drives a ball to the center.

Step 1: Stand in the center of the square. Face the target at 12 o'clock. Step out on your right foot and use your right hand, or the target stick in your right hand, to cue the dog to move to your right. Say **"<Your dog's name>, Come Bye!"**

Step 2: Click as your dog moves to your right (his left) and click again as all four of his feet come in contact with the ground target at 12 o'clock. When he is lined up perpendicular to the ball, align your position to his and cue him to **Drive!** As the ball moves around the cone, click to confirm that is what you wanted. When the ball reaches you at the center, reward him before sending him out to the next target.

Step 3: Turn and face the next ground target at 3 o'clock and repeat the process. Say **"<Your dog's name>, Come Bye!"** Click as your dog moves to your right (his left) and click again as all four of his feet come in contact with the ground target at 3 o'clock.

Step 4: When he is lined up perpendicular to the ball, align your position to his and cue him to **Drive!** As the ball moves around the cone, click to confirm that is what you wanted. When the ball reaches you at the center, reward him before sending him out to the next target. Send him out to the remaining targets at 6 o'clock and 9 o'clock in turn until the remaining balls have been brought to you at the center.

Step 5: When the final ball comes to you, cue a **Down**, reward him generously and release him with **That'll Do!**

When your dog is moving reliably around to stand on the target and driving each ball around the cone directly to you at the center successfully in 80% of his attempts, move the targets, cones and balls out in two foot increments for a total distance of sixteen feet and then repeat.

Exercise 2: Repeat Four Mat/Four Ball/Four Cone exercise, moving counterclockwise with Away to Me! drive each ball around the cone to the center

Fin moves Away to Me! and Drives a ball to the center.

Lesson #3
Exercise #1-4

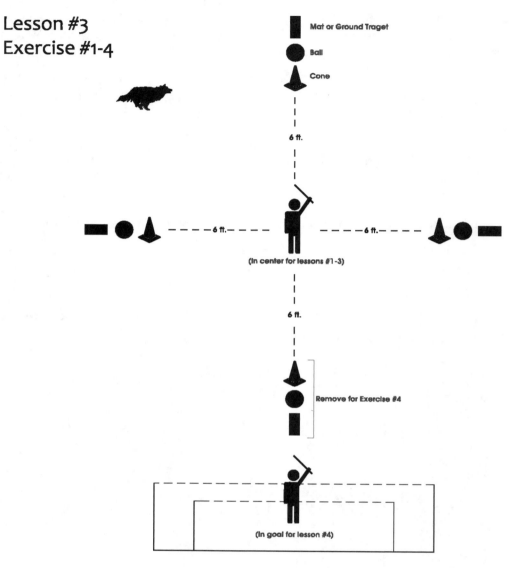

Exercise #1
Handler stands in the center. Dog will **Come Bye** to each target
and **Drive** each ball around cone to handler in the center.

Exercise #2
Handler stands in the center and transfers target stick to left hand.
Dog will move **Away to Me** to each target and **Drive** each ball
around the cone to the handler at the center.

Exercise #3
Handler stands in the center and transfers the target stick to each hand, appropriately.
Dog will move right and left, on cue, to each target as directed with
Come Bye and **Away to Me**, and **Drive** each ball around the cone to the handler at the center.

Exercise #4
Remove the ball, cone and target mat directly in front of the goal.
Handler stands in the goal and transfers the target stick to each hand, appropriately.
Dog will move to each target as directed, with **Come Bye** and **Away to Me**, and **Drive**
each ball around the cone to the handler at the goal.

Step 1: Stand in the center of the square. Face the target at 9 o'clock. Step out on your left foot and use your left hand, or the target stick in your left hand, to cue him to move to your left (his right.) Say "**<Your dog's name>, Away to Me!**"

Step 2: Click as your dog moves to your left and click again as all four of his feet come in contact with the ground target. Align your position to his and cue him to **Drive!** As the ball moves around the cone, click to confirm that is what you wanted. When the ball reaches you at the center, reward him before sending him out to the next target.

Step 3: Turn to your left again and face the next ground target, at 6 o'clock, and repeat the process. Say "**<Your dog's name>, Away to Me!**"

Click as your dog moves to your left and click again as all four of his feet come in contact with the ground target. Align your position to his and cue him to **Drive!** As the ball moves around the cone, click to confirm that is what you wanted. When the ball reaches you at the center, reward him before sending him out to the next target.

Step 4: Turn and face the next ground target, at 3 o'clock, and repeat the process. Say "**<Your dog's name>, Away to Me!**" Align your body position to his and cue him to **Drive!** As the ball moves around the cone, click to confirm that is what you wanted. When the ball reaches you at the center, reward him before sending him out to the final target at 12 o'clock.

Step 5: When the final ball comes to you, cue a **Down**, reward your dog generously and release him with **That'll Do!**

When your dog is moving reliably around to stand on the target and moving each ball around the cone directly to you at the center in 80% of his attempts, move your targets, cones and balls out in four foot increments for a total distance of sixteen feet and then repeat.

Exercise 3: Four Mat/Four Ball/Four Cone exercise, alternating moving right and left with Come Bye!/Drive! and Away to Me!/Drive! and driving each ball around the cone to you at the center

This exercise is the most difficult to accomplish since your dog will be making complete arcs around the square to each target before driving the ball to you at the center.

Step 1: With your dog in a **Down** in the **Start** position, stand in the center of the square. Face the target at 12 o'clock. Step out on your right foot and use your right hand, or the target stick in your right hand, to cue him to move to your right. Say "**<Your dog's name>, Come Bye!**"

Step 2: Click as your dog moves to your right (his left) around the cone and click again as all four of his feet come in contact with the target. Align your position to his and cue him to **Drive!** As the ball moves around the cone, click to confirm that is what you wanted and use the **Drive!** cue again (if necessary) until the ball reaches you at the center.

Step 3: Turn to your left and face the next ground target, at 9 o'clock. Step out on your left foot and use your left hand, or the target stick in your left hand, to cue him to move to your left. Say "**<Your dog's name>, Away to Me!**" Click as your dog moves to your left (his right) around the cone and click again as all four of his feet come in contact with the target. Align your position to his and cue him to **Drive!** As the ball moves around the cone, click to confirm that what you wanted and use the **Drive!** cue again (if necessary) until the ball reaches you at the center.

Step 4: Turn to your right to face the third target, at 3 o'clock. Step out on your right foot and use your right hand, or the target stick in your right hand, to cue him to move to the target to your right with **Come Bye!**

Click as your dog moves to your right around the cone and click again as all four of his feet come in contact with the ground target. Align your position to his and cue him to **Drive!** As the ball moves around the cone, click to confirm that is what you wanted and use the **Drive!** cue your dog again (*if necessary*) until the ball reaches you at the center.

Step 5: Turn left now, to face the remaining target at 6 o'clock. Step out on your left foot and use your left hand, or the target stick in your left hand, to cue him to move to your left. Say **"<Your dog's name>, Away to Me!"**

Click as your dog moves to your right (his left) around the cone and click again as all four of his feet come in contact with the ground target. Align your position to his and cue him to **Drive!** As the ball moves around the cone, click to confirm that what you wanted and use the **Drive!** cue again (*if necessary*) until the ball reaches you at the center.

Step 6: Cue a **Down**, reward your dog *generously*, and release him with **That'll Do!**

When your dog is moving reliably around in the correct direction (making a complete arc) to stand on the target and moving each ball around the cone directly to you at the center, in 80% of his attempts, move your targets, cones and balls out in four foot increments for a total distance of sixteen feet and then repeat.

Exercise 4: Three Ball/Three Cone exercise, combining Come Bye!/Drive! and Away to Me!/Drive! to move each ball laterally around the cone, before driving it to you standing within the goal area. You will move from the center to the left or right of the goal, aligning his position with yours as the ball comes forward.

Using the same field of 12 by 12 feet, remove all the ground targets. Also remove the 6 o'clock set (ball and cone), leaving only the three balls/cones that are farthest from the goal (at 12, 3 and 9 o'clock). You (the handler) will stand in the goal area, direct your dog left or right to station behind each cone/ball and cue him to **Drive!** the ball to you.

Again, begin the exercise in the **Start** position, using **Come Bye!,** to move your dog to the first target, directly in front of you (at 12 o'clock).

Three mat/ball/cone exercise set-up.

Fin will Come Bye, or move Away to Me, and Drive each ball around the obstacle to the goal.

Step 1: Stand in the center of the goal area. Face the target at 12 o'clock. Step out on your right foot and use your right hand, or the target stick in your right hand, to cue the dog to move to your right. Say **"<Your dog's name>, Come Bye!"**

Step 2: Click as your dog moves to your right to stand behind the cone and ball at 12 o'clock. Align your position to his and cue him to **Drive!** As the ball moves around the cone, click to confirm that is what you wanted and use the **Drive!** cue again (if necessary), adjusting your position in the center, right or left of the goal depending on his position and the path of the ball. Use the **Drive!** cue again (if necessary) until the ball reaches you in the goal area. Reward your dog before sending him out to the next target.

Step 3: Turn and face the next ground target, at 3 o'clock and repeat the process. Step out on your right foot and use your right hand, or the target stick in your right hand, to cue him to move to your right. Say **"<Your dog's name>, Come Bye!"** Align your position to his and cue him to **Drive!** As the ball moves around the cone, click to confirm that is what you wanted and use the **Drive!** cue again (if necessary), adjusting your position in the center, right or left of the goal depending on his alignment and the path of the ball. Use the **Drive!** cue again (if necessary) until the ball reaches you in the goal area. Reward your dog before sending him out to the last target.

Step 4: Now your dog must move left to gather the last ball, so turn to face the remaining target at 9 o'clock. Step out on your left foot and use your left hand, or the target stick in your left hand, to cue him to move to your left. Say **"<Your dog's name>, Away to Me!"** Align your position to his and cue him to **Drive!** As the ball moves around the cone, click to confirm that is what you wanted and use the **Drive!** cue again (if necessary), adjusting your position in the center, right or left of the goal depending on his alignment and the path of the ball. Use the **Drive!** cue again (if necessary) until the ball reaches you in the goal area.

Step 5: Cue your dog to lie **Down**, reward him *generously* and then release him with **That'll Do!**

When your dog is moving reliably around the cones to stand on the target in 80% of attempts while adjusting his position to yours in the goal, move your mats and cones out in two foot increments, in the same formation for a total distance of sixteen feet and then repeat.

Lesson 4

As your dog's Treibball skills increase, whether for fun or for competition, it will be necessary for him to control the entire playing field. Even though the ball-set (our flock) is placed mid-field, balls will roll (sheep will wander) and your dog will need to go further afield to gather them.

In this lesson, we introduce a barrier or obstacle that your dog must navigate around to bring a ball to you at the goal. Since these are distance exercises meant to develop more fluid movement, you will reduce your criteria in terms of distance and reward every correct placement before releasing him. As the dog's execution becomes more fluid and more precise, raise your criteria and shape and reward him for the fastest execution. Continue to click to confirm, but reward your dog only on the completion of the movement.

Exercise 1: Employing ground targets for more precise placement, you will use the (Go) Out! cue for moving the dog down-field to an obstacle at a distance, and combine it with Come Bye! and Stand. Using a field of twenty feet, your dog moves from the Start position (at 10 o'clock), runs out eight feet and moves to your right to Stand on a ground target.

A line of fencing or a solid barrier is placed in a line, ten feet out from the left-center of the goal. Place one ground target large enough for your dog to stand on, on the outside of the far end of the barrier.

Fin goes Out! Stands and Lines up outside a barrier.

Lesson #4
Exercise #1

Mat or Gound Target

20 ft

10 ft

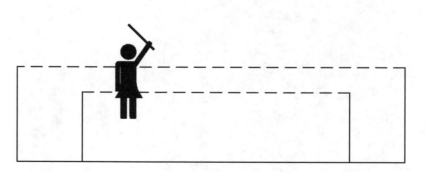

Dog moves from the Start position, out to the target mat on the outside of the barrier with the (Go)**Out/Come Bye** cue.

Step 1: With your dog in the **Start** position, stand in the left-center of the goal area. Step out on your right foot and use your right hand, or the target stick in your right hand, to cue him to move **Out!** and to your right. Say "**<Your dog's name>, (Go) Out!/Come Bye!**"

Step 2: Click as your dog moves to your right to the far end of the barrier to confirm that he has made the correct choice. Align your body position to that of your dog. Click again as all four of his feet of come in contact with the ground target on the outside of the barrier and cue him to **Stand**. If you lose his attention at this point, say "**<Your dog's name>, Watch me!**" to regain eye contact.

Step 3: Approach the target, praise your dog and toss a treat onto the mat or target. Now release your dog by saying "**That'll Do!**" and take a few steps away.

When your dog is moving reliably to the end of the barrier to stand on the target in 80% of his attempts, move your fencing/barrier line further out in five foot increments. Then repeat the exercise at each of these distances."

Your ultimate goal is to have your dog move out to the full regulation distance of the field, and stand on the mat. That is, 20 feet from the goal, for Toy breed/Small size dogs or 37.5 feet for Standard size dogs.

Exercise 2: "(Go) Out!/Away to Me!" combining cues

Now we reverse the position of the fencing, the target and the dog. Your dog will move from a **Stand** (at your right) to run out ten feet to your left (his right) and stand on the target.

Step 1: Stand in the right-center of the goal area and place your dog at your right, or in a **Stand** in the 3 o'clock position. Step out on your left foot and use your left hand, or the target stick in your left hand, to cue him to move **Out** and to your left. Say "**<Your dog's name>, (Go) Out!/Away to Me!**"

Step 2: Click as your dog moves left to the far end of the barrier, to confirm that he has made the correct choice. Align your body position to that of your dog. Click again as all four of his feet come in contact with the ground target and cue him to **Stand**.

Step 3: Approach the target, praise your dog and toss a treat onto the target. Now release your dog by saying "**That'll Do!**" and take a few steps away.

Fin will move Away to Me! and Stand on the target.

When your dog is moving reliably to the end of the barrier to stand on the target in 80% of his attempts, move your barrier out in increasing five foot increments. Repeat until your dog is moving reliably to stand on the target in 80% of his attempts to the full regulation distance of the field, 20 feet from the goal, for Toy/small breed dogs or 37.5 feet for Standard size dogs.

Lesson #4
Exercise #2

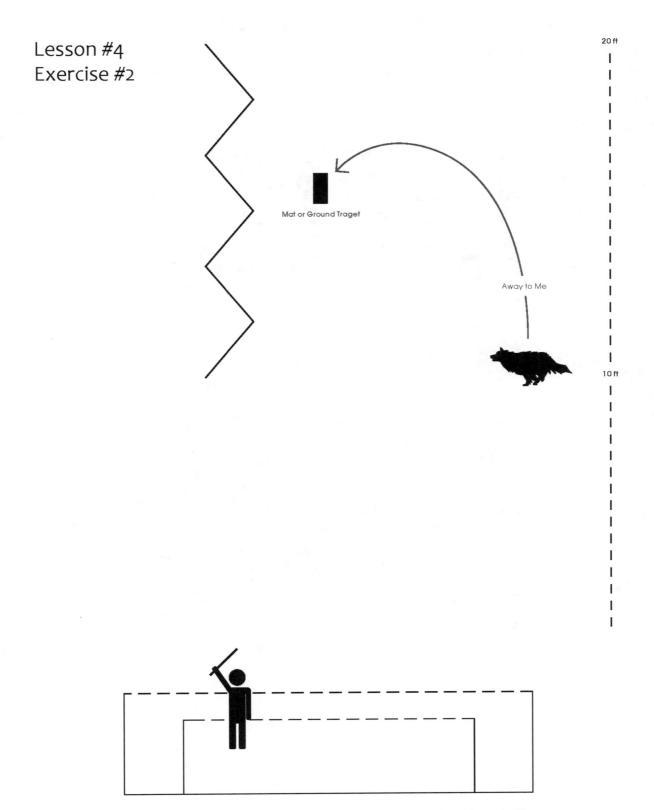

20 ft

Mat or Ground Traget

Away to Me

10 ft

Dog moves from a **Stand** in the 3 o'clock position to (Go) **Out** and **Away to Me**
to stand on the ground target on the outside of the barrier.

Exercise 3: Using the (Go) Out!/Come Bye! and Stand cues, your dog will move down-field around the obstacle in a fluid motion.

In this exercise, you will move the ground target from the outside of the barrier to the inside and repeat until your dog is quickly moving around the far end of the obstacle to stand on the inside target. A line of fencing or a solid barrier is placed in a line, ten feet out from the left-center of the goal. Place one ground target large enough for your dog to stand on inside of the far end of the barrier.

Fin will Come Bye! and Stand on the right.

Step 1: Stand in the left-center of the goal area and place your dog at your left, or in the **Start** position. Step out on your right foot and use your right hand, or the target stick in your right hand, to cue him to move **Out** and to your right. Say **"<Your dog's name>, (Go) Out!/Come Bye!"**

Step 2: Click as your dog moves around the far end of the barrier to confirm that he has made the correct choice. Align your body position to that of your dog. Click again as all four of his feet come in contact with the ground target on the inside of the barrier and cue him to **Stand.** If you lose his attention at this point, say **"<Your dog's name>, Watch me!"** to regain eye contact.

Step 3: Approach the target, praise your dog and toss a treat onto the mat or target. Now release your dog by saying **"That'll Do!"** and take a few steps away.

When your dog is moving reliably to the end of the barrier to stand on the target in 80% of his attempts, move your barrier out in increasing five foot increments. Repeat until your dog is moving reliably to stand on the target in 80% of his attempts at the proper distance on a regulation field (37 feet for Standard size dogs, 20 feet for Toy/small breeds of dogs).

Exercise 4: Your dog will respond to the (Go) Out!/Come Bye! cue by moving down-field and to your right without the barrier in place.

Now remove the fencing, leaving the ground target in the interior position in place. Your dog will respond to the "(Go) **Out!/Come Bye**" cue by moving downfield and to your right without the barrier in place.

Practice this placing your ground target five feet out from the left-center of the goal, and moving it out in five foot increments until your dog is moving reliably to stand on the target in 80% of his attempts at the proper distance on a regulation field (37 feet for Standard size dogs, 20 feet for Toy/small breeds of dogs).

Exercise 5: "(Go) Out!/Away to Me!" combining cues

Reverse the position of the fencing, the target and the dog. Your dog will move from a **Stand** (at your right), run out ten feet to your left around the barrier and stand on the target.

A line of fencing or other type solid barrier is placed in a line ten feet out from the right-center of the goal. Place one ground target large enough for your dog to stand on inside of the far end of the barrier.

Step 1: Place your dog to your right in a **Stand** at the 3 o'clock position and stand in the goal. Step out on your left foot and use your left hand, or the target stick in your left hand, to cue him to move **Out** and to your left. Say "**<Your dog's name>,** (Go) **Out!/Away to Me!**"

Step 2: Click as your dog moves left around the far end of the barrier to confirm that he has made the correct choice. Align your body position to that of your dog. Click again as all four of his feet come in contact with the ground target and cue him to **Stand**.

Step 3: Approach the target, praise your dog and toss a treat onto the target. Now release your dog by saying "**That'll Do!**" and take a few steps away.

When your dog is moving reliably around the end of the barrier to stand on the target inside in 80% of his attempts, move your fencing/barrier line out in five foot increments and repeat the exercise at each of these distances until your dog is moving reliably to the end of the barrier to stand on the target in 80% of his attempts.

Now remove the fencing, leaving the ground target in the interior position in place. Your dog will respond to the (Go) **Out!/Away to Me!** cue by moving down-field and to your left without the barrier in place. Practice this beginning five feet out from the right-center of the goal and moving the ground target out in five foot increments until your dog is moving reliably to stand on the target in 80% of his attempts.

Lesson 5

In this lesson we incorporate all the cues your dog has learned and combine the previous ground/barrier exercises with driving the ball to you at the goal from increasing distances.

Exercise #1: Combining "(Go) Out!/Away to Me" with moving one ball to the goal

A line of fencing or other solid barrier is placed in a line, 8 feet out, from the right-center of the goal. Place one ground target large enough for your dog to stand on, on the inside of the far end of the barrier. Place one ball directly in front of the mat.

Fin will move Away to Me around the barrier...

...and Drive one ball to the goal.

Step 1: Place your dog to your right in a **Stand** at the 3 o'clock position. Stand in the center-right of the goal or within the required 18 to 24 inches of the goal area. Step out on your left foot and use your left hand or the target stick in your left hand, to cue him to move out and to your left. Say **"<Your dogs' name>, (Go) Out!/ Away to Me"**

Step 2: Click as your dog moves to your left around the far end of the barrier, to confirm that he has made the correct choice. Click again as all four of his feet come in contact with the ground target and cue him to **Stand**. If you lose his attention, cue **Watch Me** to regain eye contact before adding another cue. Align your body position to that of your dog and cue your dog to **Drive**. Click to confirm as the ball moves forward to you.

Step 3: If the ball comes to your position in the goal area, cue a **Down** and reward your dog generously!

If the ball rolls at an angle or does not come directly to you at the goal line, adjust your position in the goal, to the right of center. Use the **Drive** cue again *(if necessary)* until the ball reaches you at the goal line, or redirect your dog with your directional cues **Come Bye/Drive** or **Away to Me/Drive** until the ball comes to the goal.

Step 4: When the ball comes to you at the goal line, cue a **Down** and reward your dog generously. Release your dog by saying **"That'll do!"** and take a few steps away from the goal.

Lesson #5
Exercise #1

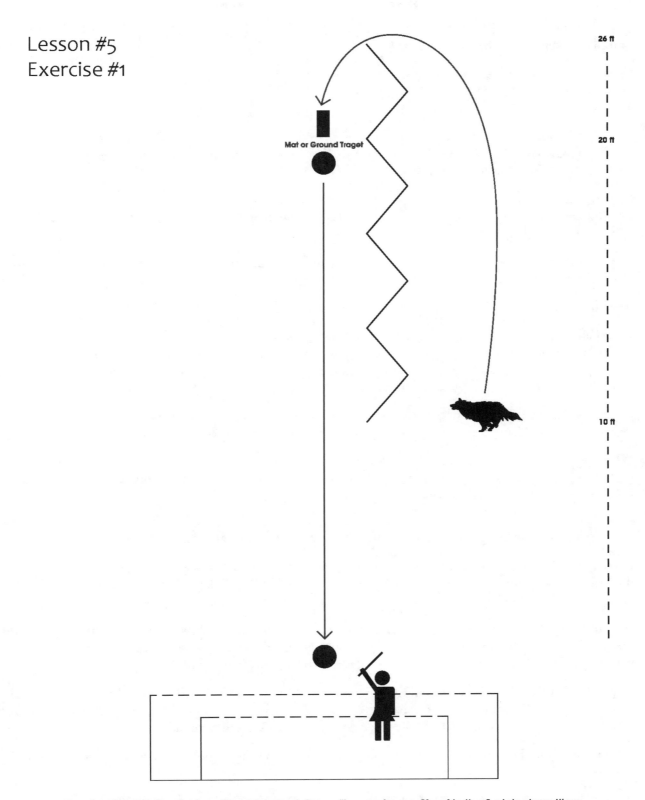

Mat or Ground Traget

26 ft

20 ft

10 ft

Handler stands in the right center of the goal. Dog will move from a **Stand** in the 3 o'clock position
to (Go) **Out** and **Away to Me** to the ground target on the inside of the barrier,
and **Drive** the ball to the handler at the goal.

Exercise #2: Now remove the fencing, leaving the ground target in the interior position, with one ball placed directly in front of the target

Using a field of twenty feet, your dog moves from a **Stand** position (at 3 o'clock) to the target. Your dog will respond to the (Go) **Out!/Away to Me** cue by moving down field and to your left, stand on the ground target, and then Drive one ball to you at the goal.

Step 1: With your dog in a **Stand** position, move back to stand in the right-center of the goal area. Step out on your left foot and use your left hand or the target stick in your left hand, to cue your dog to move **Out** and to your left. Say **"<Your dogs' name>, (Go) Out!/Away to Me."**

Step 2: Click as your dog moves to your left to confirm that he has made the correct choice. Click again as all four feet come in contact with the ground target and cue him to **Stand**. If you lose his attention, cue **Watch Me** to regain eye contact before adding another cue.

Step 3: Align your body position to that of your dog and cue your dog to **Drive**. Click to confirm as the ball moves forward to you.

If the ball comes directly to your position in the goal area, cue a **Down** and reward the dog generously!

If the ball rolls at an angle or does not come directly to you at the goal line, adjust your position in the goal, to the left or right of center depending on your dogs' position and the path of the ball. Use the **Drive** cue again (*if necessary*) until the ball reaches you or redirect your dog again with your directional cues **Come Bye/Drive or Away to Me/Drive** until the ball comes to the goal.

Step 4: When the ball comes to the goal, cue a **Down** and reward your dog generously! Release your dog by saying **"That'll do!"** and take a few steps away from the goal.

When your dog is reliably moving in a fluid motion to stand on the target and moving one ball to you at the goal, in 80% of his attempts, move your fencing/barrier line out in increasing five foot increments and repeat the exercise at each of these distances.

Exercise #3: Combining "(Go) Out!/Come Bye" with moving one ball to the goal

Reverse the direction of the barrier, the target and the dog. Your barrier is now placed in a line, 8 feet out from the left-center of the goal. Place one ground target large enough for your dog to stand on, on the inside of the far end of the fencing. Place one ball directly in front of the mat.

Step 1: With your dog in a **Down** in the **Start** position, (at 10 o'clock), move back to stand in the left-center of the goal area. Step out on your right foot and use your right hand or the target stick in your right hand, to cue your dog to move **Out** and to your right. Say **"<Your dogs' name>, (Go) Out!/Come Bye"**.

Step 2: Click as your dog moves to your right around the far end of the barrier, to confirm that he has made the correct choice. Click again as all four of his feet come in contact with the ground target and cue him to **Stand**. If you lose his attention, cue **Watch Me** to regain eye contact before adding another cue.

Step 3: Align your body position to that of your dog and cue your dog to **Drive**. Click to confirm as the ball moves forward to you.

If the ball comes directly to your position at the goal, cue a **Down** and reward your dog generously!

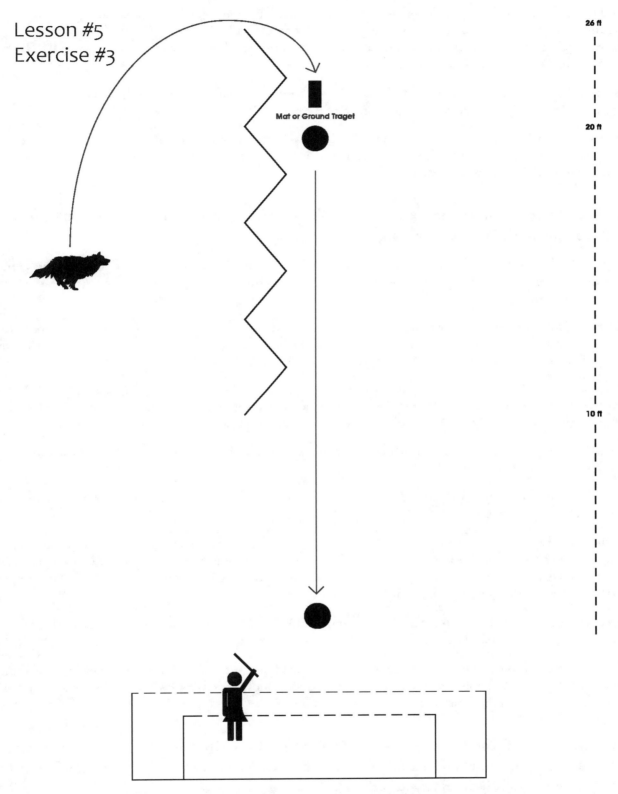

Lesson #5
Exercise #3

Mat or Ground Traget

26 ft

20 ft

10 ft

Handler stands in the left center of the goal. Dog will move from the **Start** position to (Go) **Out** and **Come Bye** to the ground target on the inside of the barrier, and **Drive** the ball to the handler at the goal.

If the ball rolls at an angle or does not come directly to you at the goal, adjust your position in the goal, to the left or right of center depending on your dogs' position and the path of the ball. Use the **Drive** cue again *(if necessary)* until the ball reaches you at the goal or redirect your dog with your directional cues **Come Bye/Drive** or **Away to Me/Drive** until the ball comes to the goal.

Step 4: When the ball comes to the goal, cue a **Down** and reward your dog generously! Release your dog by saying **"That'll do!"** and take a few steps away from the goal.

When your dog is reliably moving around the barrier in a fluid motion to stand on the target and moving one ball to you at the goal, in 80% of his attempts, move your fencing/barrier line out in increasing five foot increments and repeat the exercise at each of these distances.

Exercise #4: Now remove the fencing, leaving the ground target in the interior position, with one ball placed directly in front of the target

Using a field of 20 feet, your dog moves from the **Start** position (at 10 o'clock), will respond to the (Go) **Out!/Come Bye** cue by moving down field and to your right, stand on the ground target, and will then **Drive** one ball to you at the goal.

Step 1: With your dog in a **Down** in the **Start** position, move back to stand in the left-center of the goal area. Step out on your right foot and use your right hand or the target stick in your right hand, to cue your dog to move **Out** and to your right. Say **"<Your dogs' name>, (Go) Out!/Come Bye"**.

Step 2: Click as your dog moves to your right around the far end of the barrier, to confirm that he has made the correct choice. Click again as all four feet come in contact with the ground target and cue him to Stand. If you lose his attention, cue **Watch Me** to regain eye contact before adding another cue.

Step 3: Align your body position to that of your dog and cue your dog to **Drive**. Click to confirm as the ball moves forward to you.

If the ball comes directly to the goal, or within the 18 to 24 inches of the goal, cue a **Down** at the goal line and reward the dog generously!

If the ball rolls at an angle or does not come directly to you at the goal line, adjust your position in the goal, to the left or right of center depending on your dogs' position and the path of the ball. Use the **Drive** cue again *(if necessary)* until the ball reaches you at the goal line, or redirect your dog with your directional cues **Come Bye/Drive** or **Away to Me/Drive** until the ball comes to the goal.

Step 4: When the ball comes to the goal, cue a **Down** at the goal line and reward your dog generously! Release your dog by saying **"That'll do!"** and take a few steps away from the goal

When your dog is reliably moving in a fluid motion to stand on the target and moving one ball to you at the goal, in 80% of his attempts, move your fencing/barrier line out in increasing five foot increments and repeat the exercise at each of these distances.

Exercise 5: You will combine the cues (Go) Out!, Stand, Come Bye! or Away to Me! and Drive! to send your dog out around the barrier to a target before cueing him to Drive! one ball left or right around three small obstacles to you at the goal

This exercise combines all the skills you and your dog have acquired to this point: greater accuracy with lateral control of the ball, field positioning with large and small obstacles and better awareness of the proper alignment of your body positions to insure a more direct path to the goal. Your dog will be required to think for himself in this exercise and solve an obstacle problem without being cued.

The barrier is placed in a line, eight feet out from the left-center of the goal. Place the ground target on the opposite side of the far end of the fencing. Place one ball directly in front of the target with three traffic cones placed in a line—left, right and center. The cones should be placed approximately three feet apart and three feet out in front of the ball. The ball must be able to clear the space between the cones.

Ball-set with barrier, three cones, one target and one ball. Fin will Come Bye! to the target...

...and align his position and Drive! the ball to the goal.

Step 1: With your dog in the **Start** position, stand in the direct center of the goal area. Step out on your right foot and use your right hand, or the target stick in your right hand, to cue him to move out and to your right. Say **"<Your dog's name>, (Go) Out!/Come Bye!"**

Step 2: Click as your dog moves left around the far end of the barrier to confirm that he has made the correct choice. Click again as his feet come in contact with the ground target. When he is standing perpendicular to the ball, cue him to **Stand.** Move to the center of the goal, then cue your dog to **Drive!** and click to confirm as the ball moves forward.

Step 3: If the ball rolls up against a traffic cone, allow your dog to experiment to decide how to move it forward.

Step 4: As he drives it forward, the ball will roll at an angle around one of the cones. Align your body position in the goal to that of your dog and the path of the ball. If he overshoots the ball, use the **Back, Walk-on!** or **Line-up** cues to move him into the correct position and then redirect him with **Come Bye!/Drive!** or **Away to Me!/Drive!** until the ball comes to you at the goal.

Lesson #5
Exercise #5

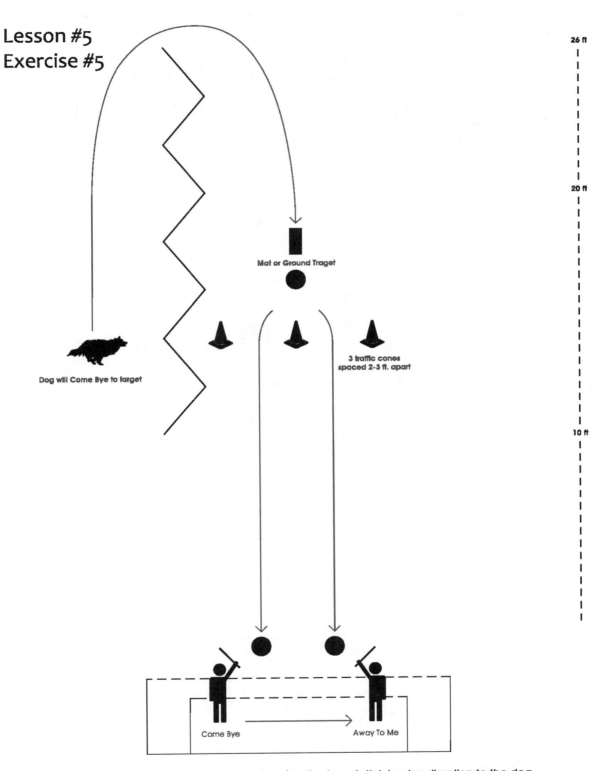

26 ft

20 ft

10 ft

Mat or Ground Traget

3 traffic cones
spaced 2-3 ft. apart

Dog will Come Bye to target

Come Bye

Away To Me

Handler moves freely within the goal, transfers the target stick to give direction to the dog
with (Go) **Out/Come Bye** or re-direct with (Go) **Out/Away to Me**, and aligns his body position
to the dog and the path of the ball. Dog will move from the **Start** position to the ground target on the inside
of the barrier, and **Drive** the ball around three small obstacles, to the handler at the goal.

Step 5: When the ball comes to you at the goal, cue a **Down** and reward your dog generously! Release him by saying **"That'll Do!"** and take a few steps away from the goal.

Now reverse the position of your fencing to the right side of the field, with the cones and target and balls on the left side of the barrier, and repeat the exercise sending your dog left, with **Away to Me!**

When your dog is moving reliably around the barrier to stand on the target in both directions with **Come Bye** and **Away to Me!** and is moving one ball to the goal in 80% of his attempts, move your fencing/barrier line out in increasing four foot increments. Repeat the exercises at each of these distances until you have achieved full field distance—20 feet out for Toy breed/Small size dogs, and 37 feet out for Standard size dogs.

Lesson 6

Now that your dog is able to command the full playing field, is lining up behind the ball and is able to move it around small ground obstacles, we introduce a larger obstacle the ball must be driven around to build your dog's problem solving ability.

As you raise our criteria in one category, adding a new element of difficulty, you need to reduce the criteria in another. In this instance you will reduce the distance to the goal. In these exercises you raise the level of difficulty by adding the larger obstacle, removing all ground targets and you (the handler) remain stationary within the goal area forcing the dog to move the ball directly to your position at the goal.

Exercise 1: Your dog will move from the Start position, run out eight feet and move one ball from behind an obstacle or barrier to the center of the field, and then will Drive! it in a straight line to you standing in the direct center of the goal

A small barrier four feet long by four feet high is placed at an angle, slightly left of center down-field, and eight feet from the goal. One ball is placed behind the barrier, with at least one foot of space between the ball and the barrier for the dog to move. The dog must **Drive!** the ball from behind the barrier on verbal cue only without being in your line of sight.

Winston aligns himself and the ball to the handler in the right-center of the goal.

Step 1: With your dog in the **Start** position, stand in the direct center of the goal area. You will align your body position to that of your dog, but *try to* remain stationary. Step out on your right foot and use your right hand, or the target stick in your right hand, to cue your dog to move out and to your right. Say "**<Your dog's name>, (Go) Out!/Come Bye!**"

Step 2: Click as your dog moves to your right to move out to the barrier. Click again as he moves behind the barrier, then cue **Away to Me!** to move him left around the ball. If he overshoots the ball, use the **Back, Walk-on!** or **Line-up** cues to move him into the correct position.

Step 3: Click to confirm when his position is aligned to the ball correctly and add the **Drive!** cue to move the ball forward out to the center of the field from behind the barrier.

Step 4: As the ball comes out from behind the barrier, align your body position within the goal area to that of your dog and the path of the ball. If necessary, cue your dog to **Drive!** again.

If the ball comes to the goal, cue him to lie Down, and reward him generously! If the ball rolls at an angle or does not come directly to you at the goal line, realign your position again and redirect your dog with **Come Bye!/Drive!** or **Away to Me!/Drive!** until the ball comes to the goal.

Lesson #6
Exercise #1

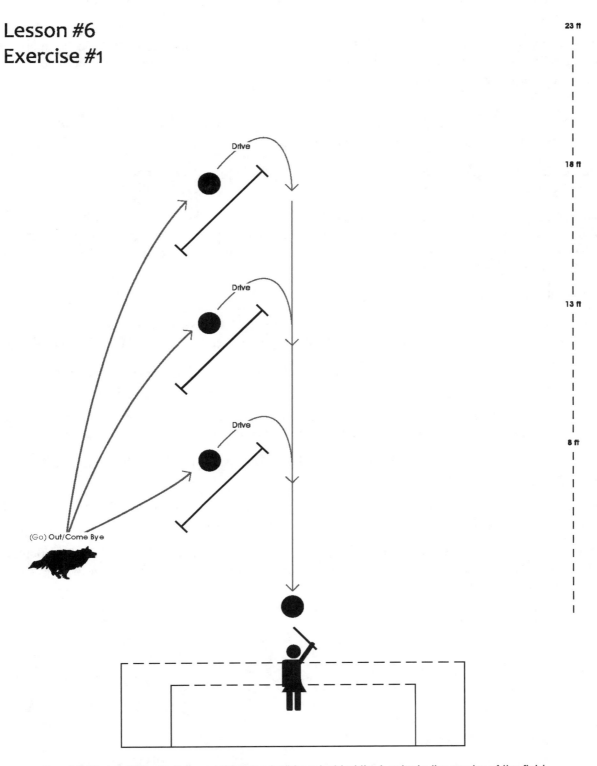

Dog will (Go) Out/Come Bye and Drive the ball from behind the barrier to the center of the field, and then to the handler at the center of the goal.

Barriers and balls move out in 5 ft. increments, to a total field distance of 18 ft.

Step 5: Cue him to lie **Down** at the goal and reward your dog generously! Release your dog by saying **"That'll Do!"** and take a few steps away from the goal.

When your dog is moving reliably behind the barrier to **Drive!** the ball out into the field in the appropriate direction in 80% of his attempts, move the barrier out in five foot increments and repeat at both thirteen and eighteen foot placements.

Exercise 2: Your dog moves from the Start position, runs out eight feet and moves one ball from behind an obstacle/barrier and will Drive it to you in the goal

In this exercise, you change position to stand in the center-left of the goal and your dog must adjust his position to match yours as he drives the ball to you.

Step 1: With your dog in the **Start** position, stand in the left-center of the goal area. You will align your body position to that of your dog's, but *try to* remain stationary. Step out on your right foot and use your right hand, or the target stick in your right hand, to cue your dog to move out and to your right. Say **"<Your dog's name>, (Go) Out!/Come Bye!"**

Step 2: Click as your dog moves to your right to move out to the barrier.

Step 3: As your dog moves behind the barrier, cue **Away to Me!** to move him left around the ball. Now cue **Drive!** to have him move the ball forward, from the left, out to the center of the field from behind the barrier.

Step 4: When the ball rolls out to the center from behind the barrier, use **Away to Me!** position your dog to to move the ball farther to the right. Align your body to the angle of your dog, behind the ball.

If your dog fails to line up perpendicular to you and the ball, use the **Watch me!** cue to gain eye contact with your dog and click on the eye contact before giving him another directional cue.

Step 5: If the ball comes forward at the correct angle (directly aligned to you in the left-center) click to confirm again before giving your dog another **Drive!** cue.

Step 6: As the ball comes to you at the left corner of the goal area, cue a **Down** and reward your dog generously. Release him by saying **"That'll Do!"** and take a few steps away from the goal.

When your dog is moving reliably behind the barrier to **Drive!** the ball out into the field in the appropriate direction in 80% of his attempts, move the barrier out in five foot increments and repeat at both thirteen and eighteen foot placements.

Lesson #6
Exercise #2

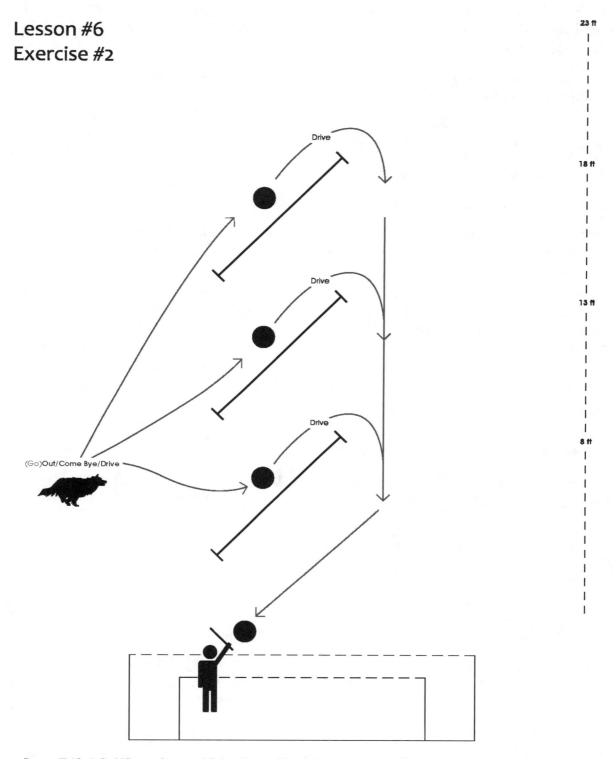

23 ft

18 ft

13 ft

8 ft

Drive

Drive

Drive

(Go)Out/Come Bye/Drive

Dog will (Go) **Out/Come Bye** and **Drive** the ball from behind a larger barrier to the center of the field, and then to the handler at the left side of the goal. Handler uses (Go) **Out/Come Bye** or transfers the target sick to the other hand to re-direct the dog with (Go) **Out/Away to Me**, to position the dog to **Drive**.

Barriers and balls move out In 5 ft. Increments, to a total field distance of 18 ft.

Exercise 3: Your dog moves from the Start position, runs out eight feet and moves one ball from behind an obstacle/barrier to the left of side of the field and will Drive! it to you standing in the right corner of the goal

Now you change your position to stand in the right corner of the goal and your dog must adjust his position to match yours as he drives the ball to you.

Step 1: With your dog in the **Start** position, move back to stand in the right-center of the goal area. You will align your body position to that of your dog, but try to remain stationary. Step out on your right foot and use your right hand, or the target stick in your right hand, to cue your dog to move out and to your right. Say **"<Your dog's name>, (Go) Out!/Come Bye!"**

Step 2: Click as your dog moves to your right (his left) to move out to the barrier.

Step 3: As he moves behind the barrier, cue (Go) **Out!/Come Bye!** to move him right around the ball, and then cue **Drive!** to have him move the ball forward from the right to the center of the field out from behind the barrier.

Step 4: When the ball rolls out to the center from behind the barrier, use your (Go) **Out/Away to Me/Drive** cue to move the ball even farther to the left, and then click to confirm as the ball moves to the left. Align your body to the angle of your dog behind the ball. If your dog fails to line up perpendicular to you and the ball, use the **Watch me!** cue to gain eye contact with your dog and click on the eye contact before giving him another verbal or directional cue.

Step 5: If the ball comes forward at the correct angle (directly aligned to you in the right corner), click to confirm again before giving your dog another **Drive!** cue.

Step 6: As the ball comes to you at the right corner of the goal area, cue a **Down** at the goal line and reward your dog generously! Release him by saying **"That'll do!"** and take a few steps away from the goal.

When your dog is moving reliably behind the barrier to **Drive!** the ball out into the field in the appropriate direction in 80% of his attempts, move the barrier out in five foot increments and repeat at both thirteen and eighteen foot placements.

Lesson #6
Exercise #3

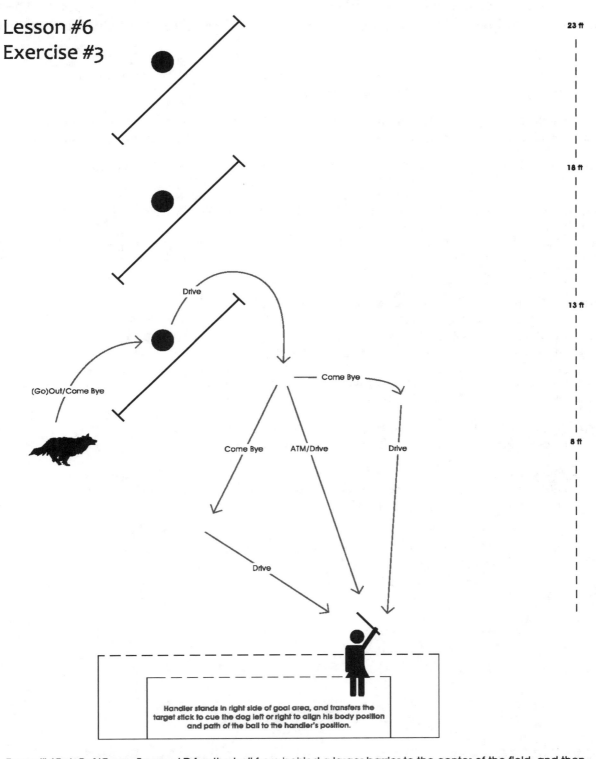

Dog will (Go) **Out/Come Bye** and **Drive** the ball from behind a larger barrier to the center of the field, and then to the handler at the right side of the goal. Handler uses (Go) **Out/Come Bye** or transfers the target sick to the other hand to re-direct the dog with (Go) **Out/Away to Me**, to position the dog to **Drive**.

Barriers and balls move out in 5 ft. increments, to a total field distance of 23 ft.

Exercise 4: Your dog moves from a Stand (in the 3 o'clock position), runs out eight feet and moves one ball from behind an obstacle/barrier to the right side of the field and will Drive it to you in the goal

In this exercise, you change position to stand in the left center or corner of the goal and your dog must adjust his position to match yours, as he drives the ball to you.

Step 1: With your dog in a **Stand** (at the 3 o'clock position), move back to stand in the left-center of the goal area. You will align your body position to that of your dogs', but try to remain stationary.

Step out on your left foot and use your left hand or the target stick in your left hand, to cue your dog to move out and to your left. Say **"<Your dogs' name>, (Go) Out!/Away to Me."**

Step 2: Click as your dog moves to your left (his right) to move out to the barrier.

Step 3: As he moves behind the barrier, cue **Away to Me, Come Bye** or **Line-up** to position him correctly to move the ball. Now cue **Drive** to have him move the ball forward, from the left out to the center of the field, from behind the barrier.

Step 4: When the ball rolls out to the center from behind the barrier, align your body to the angle in the left of the goal to that of your dog behind the ball. If your dog fails to line up perpendicular to you and the ball, use the **Watch Me!** cue to gain eye contact with your dog, and click on the eye contact before giving him another verbal cue; **Line-up, Come Bye/Drive** or **Away to Me/Drive.**

Step 5: If the ball comes forward at the correct angle (directly aligned to you in the left center) click to confirm again before giving your dog another **Drive** cue.

Step 6: As the ball comes to you at the left corner of the goal area, cue a Down at the goal line and reward your dog generously! Release him by saying **"That'll do!"** and take a few steps away from the goal

When your dog is reliably moving behind the barrier to drive the ball out into the field in the appropriate direction, in 80% of his attempts, move the barrier out, in increasing five foot increments and repeat at each of these at both thirteen and eighteen foot placements.

Lesson #6
Exercise #4

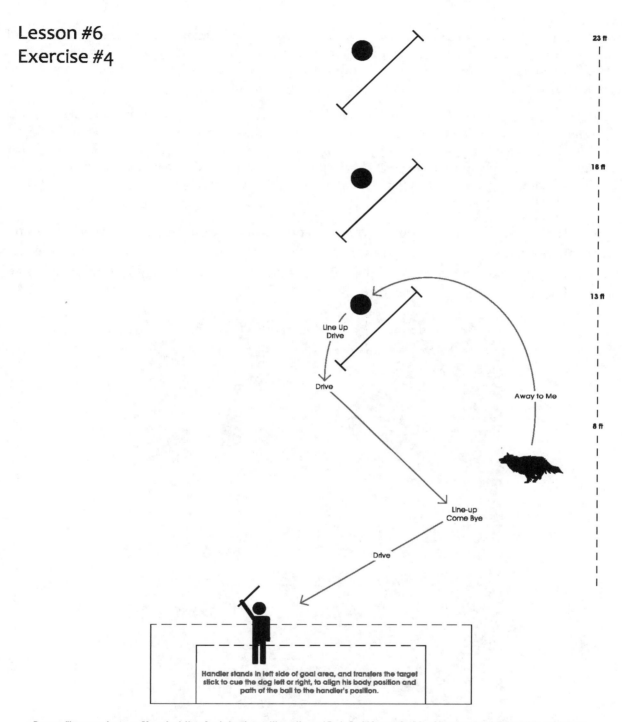

23 ft

18 ft

13 ft

Line Up
Drive

Drive

Away to Me

8 ft

Line-up
Come Bye

Drive

Handler stands in left side of goal area, and transfers the target
stick to cue the dog left or right, to align his body position and
path of the ball to the handler's position.

Dog will move from a **Stand** at the 3 o'clock position, then (Go) **Out/Away to Me**, **Line-up** and **Drive** the ball from
behind a larger barrier to the center of the field, and then to the handler at the left side of the goal. Once the ball is in
the field, handler uses **Line-up**, **Come Bye** or **Away to Me** to position the dog to **Drive**.

Barriers and balls move out in 5 ft. increments, to a total field distance of 20 ft.

Lesson 7

If we take our analogy of wandering sheep a bit further, it may happen that more than one sheep or lamb will wander farther from the flock, get separated and have to be brought back to the pen. In these exercises, a second ball and barrier provides a new challenge as you and your dog are asked to solve the problem of moving balls from behind obstructions and across the field before bringing them to the goal.

Using a total field length of twenty one feet, a solid barrier six feet long and four feet high is placed at an angle, slightly left-center down-field five feet from the goal. A second solid barrier, four feet long and four feet high is placed at an angle slightly right-center down-field seven feet from the goal. One ball is placed behind each barrier with at least one foot of space between the ball and the barrier for the dog to move. You will move within the goal area, directing your dog with fluid, multiple cues and aligning your position to that of your dog and the path of the ball.

Exercise 1: Your dog will move from the Start position, run out eight feet and move one ball from behind an obstacle or barrier to the center of the field, and will Drive! it in to you wherever you may be standing in the goal area. Your dog will then move in the opposite direction to gather another ball behind a second barrier farther up field.

Winston will Come Bye! to bring the first ball to the goal and then move Away to Me! to bring the second ball in.

Step 1: With your dog in the **Start** position, stand in the direct center of the goal area. Step out on your right foot and use your right hand, or the target stick in your right hand, to cue your dog to move out and to your right. Say **"<Your dog's name>, (Go) Out!/Come Bye!"**

Step 2: Click as your dog moves out to the barrier and click again as he moves behind the barrier, then cue **Away to Me!** to move him left around the ball. If he overshoots the ball, use the **Back** or **Line-up** cues to move him into the correct position.

Step 3: Click to confirm when his position is aligned and add the **Drive!** cue to move the ball forward from your left behind the barrier out to the center of the field. Align your position to the path of the ball as the ball comes to the goal. If the ball comes directly to the goal line, reward your dog before sending him out to gather the second ball.

Step 4: If the ball rolls at an angle or does not come directly to you at the goal, redirect your dog with (Go) **Out!/Come Bye!/Drive!** or (Go) **Out!/Away to Me!/Drive!** and align your body position to that of your dog and the path of the ball as it comes to the goal. Click as the ball comes to you at the goal and reward your dog before sending him out to gather the second ball.

Lesson #7
Exercise #1

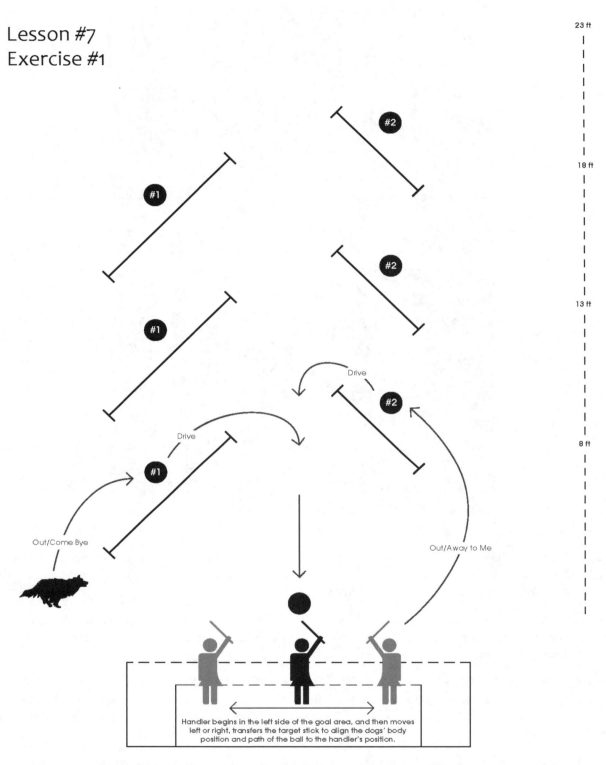

Handler begins in the left side of the goal area, and then moves
left or right, transfers the target stick to align the dogs' body
position and path of the ball to the handler's position.

Dog will move from the **Start** position, (Go) **Out/Come Bye** to **Drive** the #1 ball to the center of the field
and then to the handler at the goal. Handler then will move to the right of the goal area and cue dog
to (Go) **Out/Away to Me** to **Drive** the #2 ball to the center of the field and then to the handler at the goal.

Barriers and balls move out in 5 ft. increments, to a total field distance of 20 ft.

Step 5: The second barrier is farther up-field, on your right, so depending on your dog's current position at the goal, you can choose to send him out either right *or* left as follows:

If he's in the left or center of the goal, use your right hand, or the target stick in your right hand, to cue your dog with (Go) **Out!/Come Bye!** to send him up the middle of the field to move around the inside edge of the barrier to your right.

Or:

If he's in the right corner or right-center of the goal, use your left hand, or the target stick in your left hand, to cue your dog with (Go) **Out!/Away to Me!** to send him out around the outside edge of the barrier to your left.

Step 6: Click to confirm when his position is aligned correctly and add the **Drive!** cue to move the ball forward from your left behind the barrier out to the center of the field. If necessary, add another cue to **Drive!** and align your position to the path of the ball as it comes to the goal. If the ball rolls at an angle or does not come directly to you at the goal, redirect your dog with your directional cues **Come Bye!/Drive!** or **Away to Me!/Drive!**

Step 7: When the ball comes directly to the goal line, cue him to lie Down and reward him generously. Release him by saying **"That'll Do!"** and take a few steps away from the goal.

Repeat five times. When your dog is moving reliably behind both barriers to **Drive!** the balls out into the center of the field in the appropriate direction in 80% of his attempts, move the barriers out in five foot increments and repeat at each of these distances: five feet, ten feet and fifteen feet total placement for the exterior barrier; and seven feet, fourteen feet and twenty one feet from the exterior barrier.

Exercise 2: Your dog will gather the ball from the smaller barrier first at the far right of the field before moving to the larger barrier on the left side of the field

You move from the center to the left side of the goal, directing the dog and adjusting your position to that of your dog and the path of the ball.

You will use the same field set as before: a solid barrier six feet long and four feet high is placed at an angle slightly left of center down-field five feet from the goal. A second solid barrier, four feet long and four feet high, is placed at an angle slightly right of center down-field seven feet from the goal. One ball is placed behind each barrier with at least one foot of space between the ball and the barrier for the dog to move.

Step 1: With your dog in the Start position, stand in the left corner of the goal area. Face the far right barrier at a slight angle, and step out on your left foot. Use your right hand, or the target stick in your right hand, to cue your dog to move out and to your right. Say "**<Your dog's name>**, (Go) **Out!/Come Bye.**"

Step 2: Click as your dog moves to your right (his right) to move out to the far right barrier.

Step 3: As he moves behind the barrier, cue **Come Bye!** again to move him to the right, around the ball. Click to confirm when his position is aligned and add the **Drive!** cue to move the ball forward from behind the barrier out to the right-center of the field.

Step 4: When the ball rolls out to the center from behind the barrier, use **Come Bye!** or **Away to Me!** adding **Back, Line-up** or **Walk-on!** (if you need it) to align the dog again behind the ball before adding the **Drive!** cue to move the ball forward. Align your body to his body position behind the ball.

Lesson #7
Exercise #2

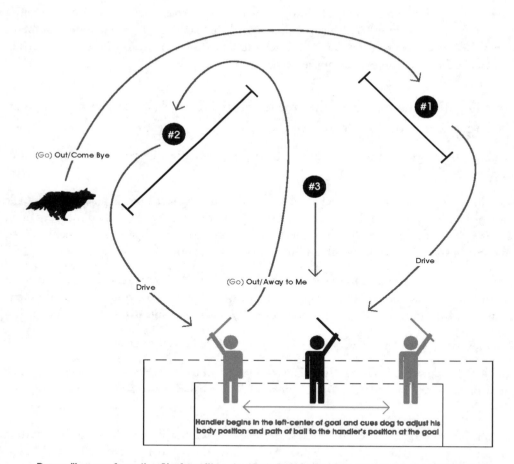

23 ft

18 ft

13 ft

8 ft

(Go) Out/Come Bye

#2

#1

#3

Drive

(Go) Out/Away to Me

Drive

Handler begins in the left-center of goal and cues dog to adjust his
body position and path of ball to the handler's position at the goal

Dog will move from the **Start** position, to (Go) **Out/Come Bye** and **Drive** the #1 ball to the center of the field
and then to the handler at the goal. Handler then moves to the right side of the goal, transferring the target
stick to send the dog left, with cue (Go) **Out/Away to Me** to gather the #2 ball on the left, Handler then returns
to the center of the goal area to direct the dog to bring in ball #3.

Step 5: If the ball comes forward at the correct angle (directly aligned to you), click to confirm again before giving your dog another **Drive!** cue. Click as the ball comes to you at the goal and reward your dog before sending him out to gather the second ball.

Step 6: The second barrier is now closer to the goal, down-field on your left, so depending on your dog's current position at the goal, you can choose to send him out either right *or* left. You will move from the left side of the goal to the center or right side, directing the dog and adjusting your position to that of your dog and the path of the ball.

If he's in the right corner or right-center of the goal, use your left hand, or the target stick in your left hand, to cue your dog with (Go) **Out!/Away to Me!** to send him out around the outside edge of the barrier to your right.

Or:

If he's in the left or center of the goal, use your right hand, or the target stick in your right hand, to cue your dog with (Go) **Out!/Come Bye!** to send him up the middle of the field to move around the inside edge of the barrier to your left.

Step 7: Click to confirm when his position is aligned correctly and add the **Drive!** cue to move the ball forward from your left behind the barrier out to the center of the field. If necessary, add another cue to **Drive!** and align your position to the path of the ball as it comes to the goal. If the ball rolls at an angle or does not come directly to you at the goal, redirect your dog with your directional cues.

Step 8: When the ball comes directly to the goal line, cue a **Down** and reward your dog generously. Release him by saying **"That'll Do!"** and take a few steps away from the goal.

When your dog is moving reliably behind both barriers to **Drive!** the balls out into the center of the field in the appropriate direction in 80% of his attempts, move the barriers out in five foot increments and repeat at each of these distances: five feet, ten feet and fifteen feet total placement for the interior barrier; and seven feet, fourteen feet and twenty one feet for the exterior barrier.

Exercise 3: Your dog will gather the balls from behind the barriers first, bring them to the center of the field, and then bring all the balls to the goal in order. You will give your dog direction and align your body position within the goal to that of your dog and the path of each ball.

Now we introduce additional balls into the field of play.

A barrier six feet long and four feet high is placed at an angle, slightly left-center down-field, five feet from the goal. A second solid barrier, four feet long and four feet high, is placed at an angle slightly right-center, farther down-field, seven feet from the goal. One ball is placed behind each barrier with at least one foot of space between the ball and the barrier for the dog to move.

Two additional balls are placed in the direct center of the field, one slightly above and to the right of the other, four feet from the goal area. The ball placed slightly above the other will be #1, designated as the point ball and will come to the goal first. The remaining balls will be #2 through 4 and be gathered in that order.

Lesson #7
Exercise #3

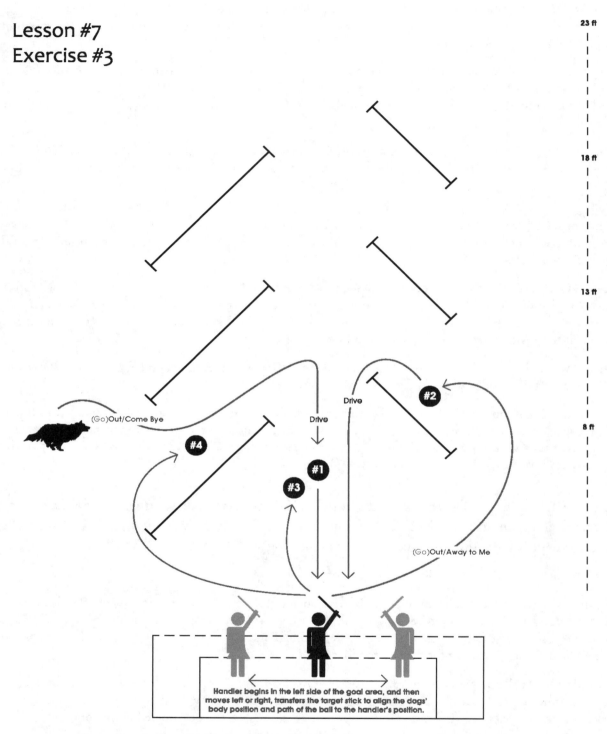

23 ft

18 ft

13 ft

8 ft

(Go)Out/Come Bye

Drive

Drive

#4

#1

#3

#2

(Go)Out/Away to Me

Handler begins in the left side of the goal area, and then
moves left or right, transfers the target stick to align the dogs'
body position and path of the ball to the handler's position.

Dog will move from the **Start** position to (Go) **Out/Come Bye** to the center of the field
and **Drive** the #1 ball to the handler at the goal. Handler then will move to the right of the goal area
and cue dog to (Go) **Out/Away to** Me to **Drive** the #2 ball from behind the short barrier
to the center of the field and then to the goal. Handler then directs the dog left or right to bring
the remaining #3 and #4 balls in, in order.

Barriers and balls move out in 5 ft. increments, to a total field distance of 23 ft.

Step 1: With your dog in a **Down** in the start position, (at 10 o'clock), stand in the right-center of the goal or within the eighteen to twenty four inches of the right corner of the goal area. Turn at a slight angle to face the interior barrier on your left. Step out on your right foot and use your right hand, or the target stick in your right hand, to cue your dog to move out and to your right. Say **"<Your dog's name>, (Go) Out!/Come Bye!"**

Step 2: Click as your dog goes out to your right to move behind the barrier. As he moves behind the barrier, use your left hand, or the target stick in your left hand, to cue **Away to Me!** to position him farther left around the ball, adding the **Back, Line-up** or **Walk-on!** cue (if you need it). Click to confirm when his position is aligned properly and add the **Drive!** cue to move the ball forward from behind the barrier out to the center of the field.

Since your dog is now accustomed to driving a ball from behind the barrier to you at the goal, we now interrupt that chain to direct him to the far barrier for the second ball.

Step 3: As the ball comes to the center of the field, cue your dog to Stand and click to confirm as he pauses in the **Stand**. If you lose his attention, say **"Watch me!"** and click on eye contact before adding your next directional cue.

Step 4: Move to the left-center of the goal and turn at a slight angle to face the down-field barrier on your right. Step out on your right foot and use your right hand, or the target stick in your right hand, to cue your dog to move out to the second barrier with (Go) **Out!/Come Bye.**

Step 5: As he moves behind the barrier, click to confirm and use your right hand, or the target stick in your right hand, to cue **Come Bye!** to move him farther right around the ball, adding the **Back, Line-up** or **Walk-on!** cue (if you need it). Click to confirm when his position is aligned correctly to the ball and add the **Drive!** cue to move the ball forward from behind the barrier out to the center of the field.

Step 6: As that ball comes to the center of the field, again cue your dog to **Stand** and click to confirm as he pauses in the **Stand**. If you lose his attention, say **"Watch me!"** and click on eye contact before adding your next directional cue.

Depending on the placement of all four balls now in the center of the field, you will need to position your dog correctly behind the point ball, slightly to the right of the ball closest to the goal.

Step 7: Use the **Come Bye!** or **Away to Me!** cues, adding **Back, Line-up** or **Walk-on!** (if you need it) to align the dog again behind the point ball before adding the **Drive!** cue to move the ball forward. Align your body to the body position of your dog and the path of the ball and click to confirm again before giving your dog another cue to **Drive!**

Step 8: Click as the point ball comes to you at the goal and reward your dog before sending him out to gather the second ball.

Step 9: Now, depending on the field position of the ball #2, you will send your dog out to bring that ball in next. Cue (Go) **Out!/Away to Me!** or (Go) **Out!/Come Bye!** to send him the correct direction to gather that ball. Click to confirm when his position is aligned correctly and add the **Drive!** cue to move the ball forward. Align your position to the path of the ball as it comes to the goal.

Step 10: When the ball comes directly to the goal line, reward your dog before sending him out to gather ball #3.

Step 11: Depending on the field position of the ball #3, you will cue either (Go) **Out!/Away to Me!** or (Go) **Out!/Come Bye!** to send him in the correct direction to gather that ball. Click to confirm when his position is aligned correctly and add the **Drive!** cue to move the ball forward. Align your position to your dog and to the path of the ball as it comes to the goal. If the ball rolls at an angle or does not come directly to you at the goal, redirect your dog with **Come Bye!/Drive!** or **Away to Me!/Drive!**

Step 12: When the ball comes directly to the goal line, reward your dog before sending him out for the final ball. Depending on the position of the last ball #4, cue (Go) **Out!/Away to Me!** or (Go) **Out!/Come Bye!** to send him in the correct direction to gather that ball.

Step 13: Click to confirm when his position is aligned correctly and add the **Drive!** cue to move the ball forward. Align your body position to that of your dog and the path of the ball as it comes to the goal.

Step 14: When the final ball comes to the goal, cue your dog to lie Down and reward him *generously* (jackpot!). Release him by saying **"That'll Do!"** and take a few steps away from the goal.

Only when your dog is moving reliably behind both barriers to **Drive!** the balls out into the center of the field and driving the four balls *in order* in 80% of his attempts, move the barriers out in five foot increments and repeat at each of these distances: five feet, ten feet and fifteen feet total placement for the interior barrier, and seven feet, fourteen feet and twenty one feet for the exterior barrier.

Only when your dog is moving reliably behind both barriers to **Drive!** the balls out into the center of the field and driving the four balls *in order* in 80% of his attempts, from the full twenty one foot length of the field, begin to vary the positions of either barrier. Move the barriers to differing positions in the field and repeat each exercise, moving barriers from the five to seven foot distance to the full field distance of fifteen to twenty one feet.

Lesson 8

At this point in your Treibball training, your dog has a full understanding of all the cues and corresponding movements that constitute truly controlled responses. He is accomplished at going down-field, moving around standing obstacles at a distance to gather the balls, and bringing them to you in order, at the goal.

The following exercises use a full playing field, that is, 75 feet long by 50 feet wide for Standard size dogs or a Teacup field of 40 feet long by 50 feet wide for Toy breed/Small size dogs.

A six foot-long barrier is placed at an angle slightly left of center down-field, twenty feet from the goal. A second solid barrier, four feet long, is placed at an angle to the far right of center, down-field twenty five feet from the goal. A third barrier a size of your choosing may be placed in the center, fifteen feet from the goal (such as a traffic cone, a hay bale or a folding chair.) One numbered ball is placed behind each barrier with at least one foot of space between the ball and the barrier for the dog to move.

The remainder of the set, five numbered balls, is placed in the triangle position at the midpoint of the field. One or two of these numbered balls may be the oddly-shaped/irregular balls. The ball placed at the point of the triangle is #1 and will be brought to the goal first.

Exercise 1: Your dog will move from the Start position and then move out to gather all the balls, in order, from down-field and behind the barriers, and Drive! each to the goal

You move within the goal area, directing your dog and aligning your body position to that of your dog and the path of the ball.

Step 1: With your dog in the Start position, stand in the direct center of the goal area. Step out on your right foot and use your right hand, or the target stick in your right hand, to cue your dog to move out and to your right. Say **"<Your dog's name>,** (Go) **Out!/Come Bye!"**

Step 2: Click as your dog moves out to **Stand** behind the point ball. If he overshoots the ball, use the **Back** or **Walk-on!** and **Line-up** cues to move him into the correct position. Click on the correct placement and add the **Drive!** cue to move the point ball forward to you at the goal. If your dog will **Drive!** the ball without being cued, simply click to confirm as the ball comes forward.

Step 3: Align your position to your dog and the path of the ball as the ball comes to the goal. If the point ball comes directly to the goal line, reward your dog before sending him out to gather the second ball.

If the ball rolls at an angle or does not come directly to you at the goal, and align your position to your dog's position and to the path of the ball and cue **Drive!** again *without* adding any further directional cues (**Come Bye!/Drive** or **Away to Me!/Drive!**).

When the point ball comes directly to your position at the goal line, reward your dog before sending him out to gather the second ball.

Step 4: The second ball lies behind the far barrier, twenty feet from the goal on your right, so move to the left corner of the goal area. Turn slightly to face the barrier. Step out on your left foot and use your left hand, or the target stick in your left hand, to cue your dog with (Go) **Out!/Away to Me!** to send him to the barrier.

Step 5: Click to confirm when his position is aligned with the ball and add the **Drive!** cue to move the ball forward from behind the barrier out to the center of the field.

If the ball rolls at an angle or does not come directly to you at the goal, align your position to your dog and to the path of the ball and cue **Drive!** again *without* adding any further directionals. Align your position to the path of the ball as it comes to the goal.

Lesson #8
Exercise #1

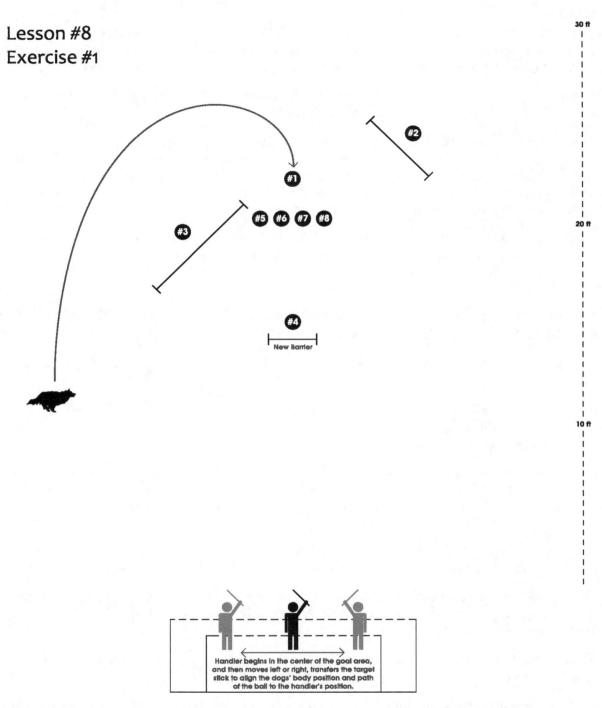

Dog will move from the **Start** position to (Go) **Out/Come Bye** to the center of the field and **Drive** the #1 ball
to the handler at the goal. Handler then will move to the right of the goal area and cue dog to (Go) **Out/Away to Me**
to **Drive** the #2 ball from behind the short barrier to the center of the field and then to the goal.
Handler then moves within the goal, directing the dog to bring the remaining 6 balls in, in order.

Barriers and balls move out in 10 ft. increments to a total field distance of 30 ft.

Step 6: When the #2 ball comes directly to your position at the goal line, reward your dog before sending him
out to gather the third ball.

Step 7: Ball #3 lies behind the long barrier, down-field on your left, twelve feet from the goal. Move to the right corner of the goal, and cue (Go) **Out!/Come Bye!** Click to confirm when his position is aligned with the ball and add the **Drive!** cue to move the ball forward from behind the barrier out to the center of the field. If necessary, use the **Back, Walk-on!** or **Line-up** cues to move him into the correct position and click on the correct placement.

Step 8: Align your body position to that of your dog and the path of the ball, and add the **Drive!** cue to move the point ball forward to you at the goal. If your dog will **Drive!** the ball without being cued, simply click to confirm as the ball comes forward. When the #3 ball comes directly to your position at the goal line, reward your dog before sending him out to gather the fourth ball.

Step 9: Ball #4 is directly in the center of the field, behind the new barrier, so use your discretion whether to send your dog left or right to gather it. As the ball comes from behind the barrier, align your body position to that of your dog and the path of the ball, and cue your dog to **Drive!** again, if necessary. As the ball comes to you at the goal, reward your dog before sending him out to gather the fifth ball.

Step 10: Balls 5 through 8 remain in a line, at the center of the field, 35 feet from the goal area. Using your directional cues, bring in the remaining balls in order. Balls #5 and #6 on the left of the line can be brought with (Go) **Out!/Come Bye!** and #7 and #8 on the right side of the line can be brought in with (Go) **Out!/Away to Me!** If that's just too easy, you can alternate sending your dog left and then right using (Go) **Out!/Come Bye!** for # 5, (Go) **Out!/Away to Me!** for #6, then (Go) **Out!/Come Bye!** for #7, and (Go) **Out!/Away to Me!** for #8.

Step 11: When the final ball comes to the goal, cue your dog to lie **Down** and reward him generously. Release your dog by saying **"That'll Do!"** and take a few steps away from the goal.

When your dog is reliably completing 80% of his attempts, begin to move the balls and barriers for this from the goal area and vary your rate of reward. Begin by rewarding your dog on every other completion or then on every third completion, moving up to only rewarding your dog on the completion of the entire exercise.

Exercise 2: Your dog will move from the Start position and then move out to gather all the balls, in order, from down-field and behind the barriers, and will Drive! each to the goal

We now move our barriers farther afield and present more random numbering of the balls.

The six foot-long solid barrier is placed at an angle, slightly right of center down-field, twelve feet from the goal. A second solid barrier, four feet long, is placed at an angle to the far left of center, up-field fifteen feet from the goal. A third barrier, the size of your choosing, may be placed anywhere in the field six to ten feet from the goal. One numbered ball is placed behind each barrier with at least one foot of space between the ball and each barrier for the dog to move. The remainder of the set, five numbered balls, is placed at random in the field. One or two of these numbered balls may be the oddly-shaped, irregular balls. The point ball is placed farthest down-field and will be brought to the goal first.

You will move within the goal area, right, left or center, directing your dog and aligning your body position to that of your dog and the path of the ball.

Step 1: With your dog in the **Start** position, stand in the direct center of the goal area. Step out on your right foot and use your right hand, or the target stick in your right hand, to cue your dog to move out and to your right. Say **"\<Your dog's name>, (Go) Out!/Come Bye!"**

Step 2: When your dog reaches the correct position down-field to stand behind the point ball, click on the correct placement and align your body position to that of the dog and the path of the ball. Add the **Drive!** cue to move the point ball to the center of the field. If your dog will **Drive!** the ball without being cued, simply click to confirm as the ball comes forward.

If the ball rolls at an angle or does not come directly to you at the goal, redirect your dog with **Come Bye!/Drive!** or **Away to Me!/Drive!** and align your body position to that of your dog and the path of the ball as the ball comes to the goal. If necessary, use the **Back, Walk-on!** or **Line-up** cues to move him into the correct position and click on the correct placement before adding the cue to **Drive!**

As the point ball comes directly to you at the goal line, reward your dog before sending him out to gather the second ball.

Step 3: In the diagram, the #2 ball is an oddly-shaped/irregular ball down-field on your far right. Use your directional cues to send your dog out in the appropriate direction. Depending on the weighted end of that ball, prepare to shift your position quickly to direct that ball to the goal. Click to confirm when his position is aligned with the ball and add the **Drive!** cue to move the ball forward. Align your position to the path of the ball as it comes to the goal. Reward your dog before sending him out to gather the #3 ball.

Step 4: Ball #3 is placed mid-field twenty feet from the goal, so you may send him far out/right with (Go) **Out!/Come Bye!** or though the center of the field by going out/left with (Go) **Out!/Away to Me!** Click to confirm when his position is aligned with the ball and add **Drive!**

If your dog will **Drive!** the ball without being cued, simply click to confirm as the ball comes forward. If the ball does not come directly to the goal, redirect your dog and reposition yourself in the goal. When the #3 ball comes directly to your position at the goal line, reward your dog before sending him out to gather the #4 ball.

Step 5: Ball #4 is down-field ten feet from the goal and behind the long barrier, so align yourself in the right-center of the goal and use (Go) **Out!/Come Bye!** to send your dog to your right to bring that ball. Click to confirm when his position is aligned and add **Drive!** As the ball comes from behind the barrier, align your body position to that of your dog and the path of the ball and cue your dog to **Drive!** again if necessary.

If the ball rolls at an angle or does not come directly to you at the goal, redirect your dog with **Come Bye!/Drive!** or **Away to Me!/Drive!** and align your body position to that of your dog and the path of the ball as it comes to the goal.

When the #4 ball comes directly to your position at the goal line, reward your dog before sending him out to gather the #5 ball.

Step 6: Ball #5 lies behind the shorter, solid barrier fourteen feet to the right-center of the goal area, You may send him far out/right with **Come Bye!** or around the outside of the field, with (Go) **Out!/Away to Me!** Click to confirm when his position is aligned with the correct ball and add **Drive!** As the ball comes from behind the barrier, align your body position to that of your dog and the path of the ball and cue your dog to **Drive!** again if necessary. When the #5 ball comes directly to your position at the goal line, reward your dog before sending him out to gather the #6 ball.

Step 7: Ball #6 is also on your right, behind the new, small barrier ten feet from the goal. Since #8 still lies in the center of the field, another (Go) **Out!/Away to Me!** will send him behind the barrier without disturbing the ball at the center. Click to confirm when his position is aligned with the ball and add the cue to **Drive!** As the ball comes from behind the barrier, align your body position to that of your dog and the path of the ball and cue your dog to **Drive!** again if necessary.

If the ball rolls at an angle or does not come directly to you at the goal, redirect your dog with **Come Bye!/Drive!** or **Away to Me!/Drive!** and align your body position to that of your dog and the path of the ball as the ball comes to the goal. If necessary, use the **Back, Walk-on!** or **Line-up** cues to move him into the correct position, and click on the correct placement before adding the cue to Drive!

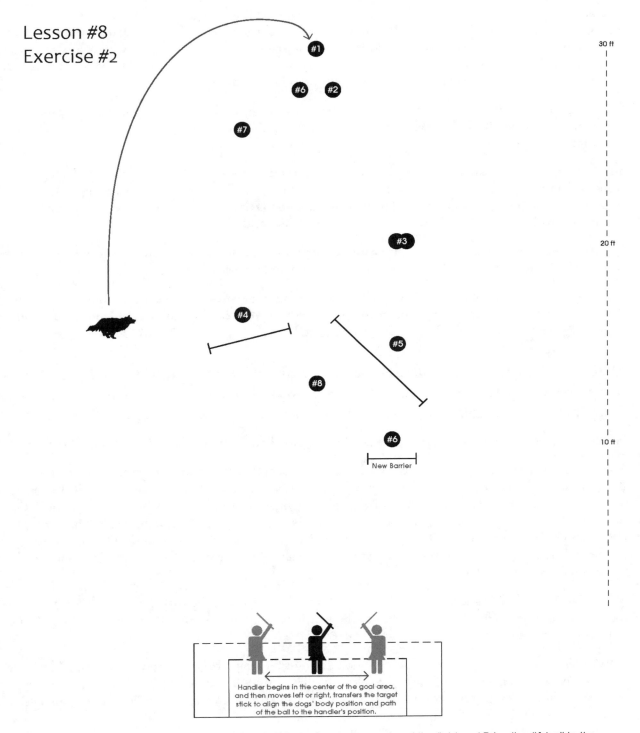

Lesson #8
Exercise #2

New Barrier

Handler begins in the center of the goal area, and then moves left or right, transfers the target stick to align the dogs' body position and path of the ball to the handler's position.

Dog will move from the **Start** position to (Go) **Out/Come Bye** to the center of the field and **Drive** the #1 ball to the handler at the goal. Handler then moves within the goal, directing the dog to bring the 7 remaining balls in, in order. Ball-set may include 1 or 2 odd/irregular shaped balls.

When the #6 ball comes directly to your position at the goal line, reward your dog before sending him out to gather the #7 ball.

Step 8: The #7 ball lies down-field on your left at twenty two feet from the goal, so move to the right-center of the goal area and use (Go) **Out!/Come Bye!** to send your dog out to bring that ball. Click to confirm when his body position is aligned with the ball and add **Drive!** Align your body position to that of your dog and the path of the ball, and cue your dog to **Drive!** again, if necessary. When the #7 ball comes directly to your position at the goal line, reward your dog before sending him out to gather the last ball.

If the ball rolls at an angle or does not come directly to you at the goal, redirect your dog with **Come Bye!/ Drive!** or **Away to Me!/Drive!** and align your body position to that of your dog and the path of the ball as the ball comes to the goal.

Step 9: Only #8 remains in the center of the field at nine feet from the goal. Depending on your dog's position at the goal when #7 comes in, use your discretion whether to send your dog left or right to bring it in. Click to confirm when his body position is aligned with the ball and add **Drive!** Align your body position to that of your dog and the path of the ball, and cue your dog to **Drive!** again if necessary.

Step 10: When the final ball comes to the goal, cue your dog to lie **Down** and reward him generously. Release your dog by saying **"That'll Do!"** and take a few steps away from the goal

When your dog is reliably completing 80% of his attempts, begin to raise your criteria/vary your rate of reward. Begin by rewarding your dog on every other completion or then on every third completion, moving up to only rewarding your dog on the completion of the entire exercise.

Exercise 3: Using the full field of play and numbered balls, your dog will bring the point ball in first, followed by the remaining balls in succession. You will move fluidly within the goal area, from center, right or left, aligning your body position to that of your dog and the path of the ball.

Finally, you "up the ante" by introducing three new barriers in addition to the two you've already placed in the field.

The four or six foot-long solid barrier is placed at an angle, slightly left of center, down-field, fifteen feet from the goal. A small, solid barrier, four feet long, is placed at an angle, to the far left of center, up-field seventeen feet from the goal. A third barrier, the size of your choosing may be placed to the right-center of the goal. One numbered ball is placed behind each barrier, with at least one foot of space between the ball and barrier for the dog to move. The remainder of the set, five numbered balls, are placed at random in the field. One or two of these numbered balls may be the oddly-shaped/irregular balls. The point ball is placed farthest down-field and will be brought to the goal first.

Step 1: With your dog in the **Start** position, stand in the direct center of the goal area. Step out on your right foot and use your right hand, or the target stick in your right hand, to cue your dog to move out and to your right. Say **"<Your dog's name>, (Go) Out!/Come Bye!"**

Step 2: When your dog reaches the correct position down-field to stand behind the point ball, click on the correct placement and align your body position to that of the dog and the path of the ball. Add the **Drive!** cue to move the point ball to the center of the field. If your dog will **Drive!** the ball without being cued, simply click to confirm as the ball comes forward.

If the ball rolls at an angle or does not come directly to you at the goal, redirect your dog with **Come Bye!/ Drive!** or **Away to Me!/Drive!** and align your body position to that of your dog and the path of the ball as the ball comes to the goal If necessary, use the **Back, Walk-on!** or **Line-up** cues to move him into the correct position, and click on the correct placement before adding the cue to **Drive!**

Lesson #8
Exercise #3

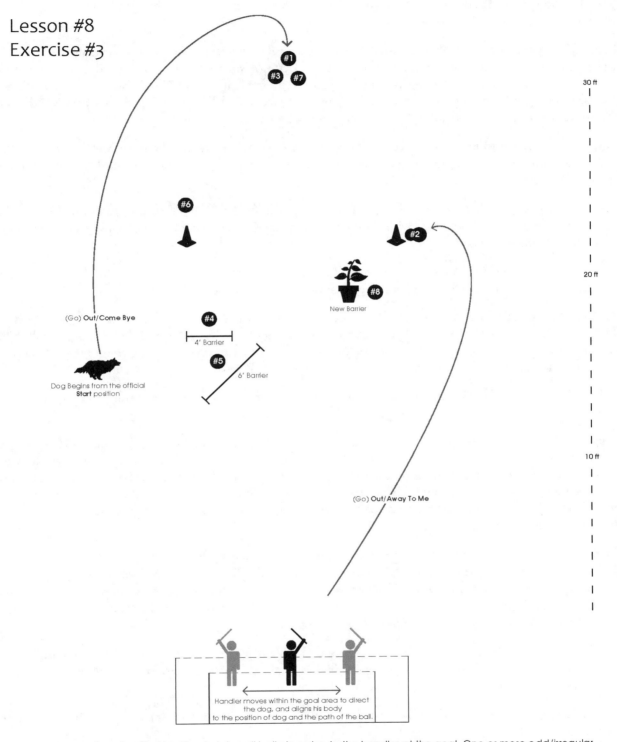

30 ft

20 ft

10 ft

#1

#3 #7

#6

#2

#8

New Barrier

(Go) Out/Come Bye

#4

4' Barrier

#5

6' Barrier

Dog Begins from the official **Start** position

(Go) Out/Away To Me

Handler moves within the goal area to direct the dog, and aligns his body to the position of dog and the path of the ball.

Dog will move from the **Start** position to bring all balls, in order, to the handler at the goal. One or more odd/irregular shaped balls may be used or substituted for regulation balls.

Step 3: As the point ball comes directly to you at the goal line, reward your dog before sending him out to gather the second ball.

Step 4: In the diagram, the #2 ball is beside a traffic cone twenty two feet from the goal, down-field on your far right. Move to the right–center of the goal and use (Go) **Out!/Away to Me!** to send your dog out around the right side. Click to confirm when his position is aligned with the ball and add the **Drive!** cue to move the ball forward toward the center of the field. Depending on the trajectory of that ball, the path may be down the center of the field or may be down the right side, and the ball may rest near or dislodge ball #8 directly in its path.

You will need to reposition and redirect your dog with **Come Bye!/Drive!** or **Away to Me!/Drive!** and align your body position to that of your dog and the path of the ball as the ball comes to the goal. Reward your dog before sending him out to gather the #3 ball.

Step 5: Ball #3 is placed at the far back of the field, at thirty three feet from the goal, so you move to the right-center of the goal to send him right with (Go) **Out!/Come Bye!** Click to confirm when his position is aligned with the ball and add **Drive!**

If your dog will **Drive!** the ball without being cued, simply click to confirm as the ball comes forward. If the ball does not come directly to the goal, redirect your dog and reposition yourself in the goal.

If the ball rolls at an angle or does not come directly to you at the goal, redirect your dog with **Come Bye!/Drive!** or **Away to Me!/Drive!** and align your body position to that of your dog and the path of the ball as the ball comes to the goal. If necessary, use the **Back, Walk-on!** or **Line-up** cues to move him into the correct position, and click on the correct placement before adding the cue to Drive!

When the #3 ball comes directly to your position at the goal line, reward your dog before sending him out to gather the #4 ball.

Step 6: Ball #4 is down-field, on your left, eighteen feet from the goal, behind the small barrier, so align yourself in the right-center of the goal and use (Go) **Out!/Come Bye!** to send your dog to out and your right to bring that ball. Click to confirm when his position is aligned with the correct ball and add **Drive!** As the ball comes from behind the barrier, align your body position to that of your dog and the path of the ball, and cue your dog to **Drive!** again, if necessary. When the #4 ball comes directly to your position at the goal line, reward your dog before sending him out to gather the #5 ball.

Step 7: Ball #5 lies behind the solid barrier at four feet to the left-center of the goal area. You may choose to send him on a short outside path to move the ball to the center with (Go) **Out!/Come Bye!,** or around the upper inside edge of the barrier with (Go) **Out!/Away to Me!** Click to confirm when his position is aligned and add the **Drive!** cue. As the ball comes from behind the barrier, align your body position to that of your dog and the path of the ball, and cue your dog to **Drive!** again if necessary.

If the ball rolls at an angle or does not come directly to you at the goal, redirect your dog with **Come Bye!/Drive!** or **Away to Me!/Drive!** and align your body position to that of your dog and the path of the ball as the ball comes to the goal.

When the #5 ball comes directly to your position at the goal line, reward your dog before sending him out to gather the #6 ball.

Step 8: Ball #6 is also on your upper left, behind a traffic cone twenty four feet from the goal. Since the center of the field is clear, use (Go) **Out!/Come Bye!** move the dog around the cone. Click to confirm when his position is aligned with the ball and add **Drive!** As the ball comes from behind the cone, align your body position to that of your dog and the path of the ball, and cue your dog to **Drive!** again, if necessary.

When the #6 ball comes directly to your position at the goal line, reward your dog before sending him out to gather the #7 ball.

Step 9: Ball #7 is the farthest down-field at right-center, thirty three feet from the goal. Move to the right-center of the goal area and use (Go) **Out!/Come Bye!** to send your dog out to bring that ball. Click to confirm when his body position is aligned with the ball and add **Drive!** Align your body position to that of your dog and the path of the ball, and cue your dog to **Drive!** again if necessary. When the #7 ball comes directly to your position at the goal line, reward your dog before sending him out to gather the last ball.

Step 10: Only #8 remains, mid-field, behind the third new barrier, at nineteen feet from the goal. Move to the right–center of the goal and use (Go) **Out!/Away to Me!** to send your dog out around the right side. Click to confirm when his position is aligned with the ball and add the **Drive!** cue to move the ball forward toward the center of the field. Click to confirm when his body position is aligned with the ball and add **Drive!**

Align your body position to that of your dog and the path of the ball and cue your dog to **Drive!** again, if necessary.

Step 11: When the final ball comes to the goal, cue your dog to lie Down and reward him generously. Release your dog by saying **"That'll Do!"** and take a few steps away from the goal

Repeat five times. When your dog is reliably completing 80% of his attempts, begin to raise your criteria/vary your rate of reward. Begin by rewarding your dog on every other completion or then on every third completion, moving up to only rewarding your dog on the completion of the entire exercise.

WOW! Look how far you and your dog have come!!!
Congratulations on your excellent teamwork!!

Lesson 9

Our final training session represents three new scenarios for Advanced Treibball and a chance to test your problem solving skills: a final exam for you! Assess the field presented in the diagrams, note what you will do, what cues you will use and then track the successful completion of your session. Next, practice those signals or cues and time the execution of the exercise, so you have a realistic idea of what cues or movements you and your dog will need to tighten up for more fluid movements and better timing.

Exercise 1

Field set-up: (What are the most challenging placements in this field? What cues will you use, in what order?)

Handler's position in the goal: (Where will you stand in the goal area to provide the most accurate direction to your dog?)

Ball position: (What is the relationship in the way the balls are placed?)

Dog position: (What is the most efficient way for your dog to move the balls forward—his most direct path to the goal?)

Step 1: _____

_____

Step 2: _____

_____

Step 3: _____

_____

Step 4: _____

_____

Step 5: _____

_____

Step 6: _____

_____

Step 7: _____

_____

Step 8: _____

_____

Total time for execution: _____

Additional ideas or notes: _____

_____

_____

Lesson #9
Exercise #1

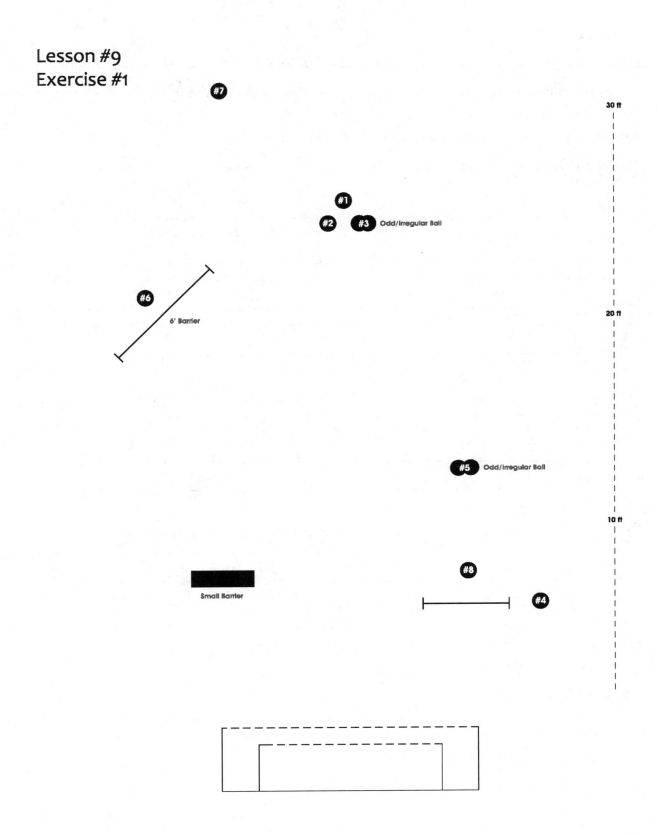

Exercise 2

Field set-up: (What are the most challenging placements in this field? What cues will you use, in what order?)

Handler's position in the goal: (Where will you stand in the goal area to provide the most accurate direction to your dog?)

Ball position: (What is the relationship in the way the balls are placed?)

Dog position: (What is the most efficient way for your dog to move the balls forward—his most direct path to the goal?)

Step 1: _____
_____

Step 2: _____
_____

Step 3: _____
_____

Step 4: _____
_____

Step 5: _____
_____

Step 6: _____
_____

Step 7: _____
_____

Step 8: _____
_____

Step 9: _____
_____

Step 10: _____
_____

Total time for execution: _____

Additional ideas or notes: _____
_____
_____

Lesson #9
Exercise #2

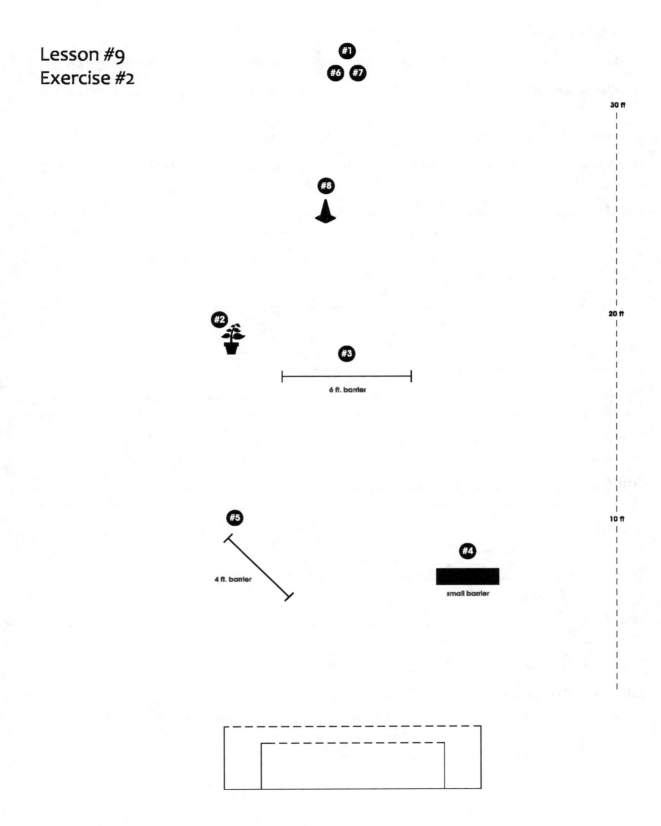

Exercise 3

Field set-up: (What are the most challenging placements in this field? What cues will you use, in what order?)

Handler's position in the goal: (Where will you stand in the goal area to provide the most accurate direction to your dog?)

Ball position: (What is the relationship in the way the balls are placed?)

Dog position: (What is the most efficient way for your dog to move the balls forward—his most direct path to the goal?)

Step 1: _____

_____

Step 2: _____

_____

Step 3: _____

_____

Step 4: _____

_____

Step 5: _____

_____

Step 6: _____

_____

Step 7: _____

_____

Step 8: _____

_____

Step 9: _____

_____

Step 10: _____

_____

Total time for execution: _____

Additional ideas or notes: _____

_____

_____

Lesson #9
Exercise #3

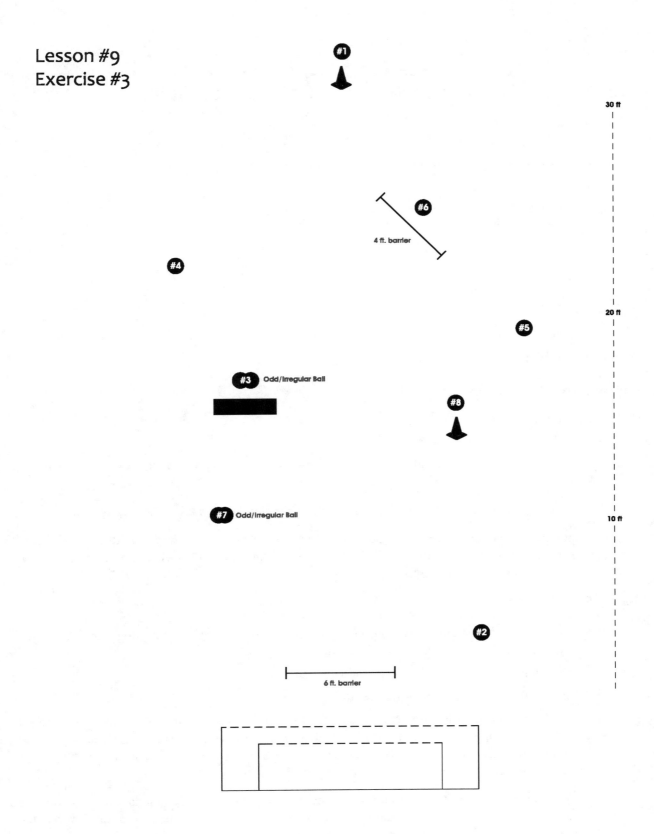

American Treibball Association
Sanctioned Trial and Competition Rules
For 2013
Revised/Approved by the membership September 5, 2012

A. Membership

Applying For Membership

1. Membership within the ATA is a privilege. To compete in, or host, sanctioned competitions, the individual must be a current member.

2. Application for membership may be made by using the contact form on our website, www.americantreibballassociation.org

3. The name appearing on the membership shall be the exact same name used for any registration.

4. By applying for membership, the applicant automatically agrees to be bound by and abide by the By-Laws and Rules and Regulations of the ATA. The ATA Board of Directors shall review and determine annual registration, event and licensing fees.

Types of Membership

1. **Level I—Adult**. Restricted to one person. This is a requirement to compete with a dog at any ATA sanctioned trial or competition, regardless of other memberships held.

   a. This membership is carried in the individual's legal name.

   b. This membership is for one person over the age of 18 years.

   c. Level I members are full voting members of the ATA, and will receive the Introduction to Treibball curriculum, a copy of the ATA Bylaws, and the Sanctioned Trial/Competition rules, in addition to training tips and notification of events and competitions. To join at Level I, click here to fill out the contact form on our website www.americantreibballassociation.org

2. **Level I—Junior Handler.** This membership is for young dog owners who want to train and compete with a dog. Restricted to one person under the age of 18. This is a requirement to compete with a dog at any ATA sanctioned trial or competition, regardless of other memberships held.

a. This membership is carried in the individual's legal name. Young competitors under the age of 18 years may compete in the following age groups:

- ○ 8-10
- ○ 11-13
- ○ 14-17

The age of the Junior Handler on January 1 of the year of registration, determines the age category that handler will compete in, for that calendar year.

b. Every Junior Handler must be accompanied by a parent or responsible adult, at all times during competitions.

c. Every Junior Handler must demonstrate to competition hosts that they can control their dog in an off-leash environment.

d. Junior Handlers are not voting members of the association. To join at Level I, Junior Handler, click here to fill out the contact form on our website www.americantreibballassociation.org

3. **Level II: Professional Trainer**. For positive reinforcement trainers who want to add Treibball classes to their existing class schedule, or who wish become a certified ATA regional/local Treibball trainer.

a. Level II members are full voting members of the Association, and will receive the full ATA curriculum, the organizations' Bylaws and the current Sanctioned Trial/Competition Rules.

b. Level II and Level III members are eligible to attend the trainer certification academy, and after completion will be listed on our website as a Certified American Treibball Trainer (CATT).

We require an IRS EIN or Tax ID number, your training website URL, and two professional references: one from a practicing veterinarian in your area who refers training clients to you, and one from a business colleague or a training client. Send this information through the Contact Form on our website, www.americantreibballassociation.org first, before registering. Once we approve your application, you will be notified to register for membership. Do not fill out the registration form or pay for membership until you are notified.

4. **Level III: Regional/Local Dog Training Club, Breed Club, Training Association or Training facility**

a. Level III members are full voting members of the ATA, and must have at least one positive reinforcement trainer dedicated to the sport.

b. Clubs, associations or facilities may send a representative to annual meetings. Clubs, associations or facilities will receive the full ATA curriculum, the Bylaws and Sanctioned Trial/Competition Rules.

c. Clubs associations or facilities are allowed to hold sanctioned competitions, and may send a representative to the trainer certification academy.

We require an IRS EIN or Tax ID number, your training website URL, and two professional references; one from a practicing veterinarian in your area who refers training clients to you, and one from a business colleague or a training client. Send this information through the Contact Form on our website, www.americantreibballassociation.org first, before registering. Once we approve your application, you will be notified to register for membership. Do not fill out the registration form or pay for membership until you are notified.

Membership Fees

1. Membership in the ATA is based on the calendar year. Renewals are due December 31 of each year.

2. Fees paid are non-refundable or non-transferable. Refer to the Current Fee Schedule for Level I, II and III memberships, which are listed on the website

B. General Operating Rules, ATA Authority Concerning Registration and Rules.

1. The rules and registration numbers of the Association take precedence over those of any other Association.

2. The ATA reserves the right to make any changes in these rules, regulations, standards, or requirements as deemed at any time, to be in the best interest of the ATA and the sport of Treibball.

3. Every approved competition and every person participating therein is subject to the Bylaws and Sanctioned Trial and Competition Rules of the ATA.

4. All members will be notified of any votes needed to change the rules, policies and procedures through email and through the members' discussion group, americantreibballassociation.com@yahoogroups.com

Any changes made become effective January 1 of the following year.

C. General Registration Responsibility

1. The person submitting the registration is responsible for the accuracy of all information submitted.

2. The owner of the dog must have a membership in the exact name as it is to appear on the dog's registry.

3. Dogs competing must be registered in the correct class, size and age-appropriate categories.

   Classes, sizes and ages are as follows:

   Classes:
   - ATA Beginner
       - Division A—use of a clicker is allowed
       - Division B—only verbal, whistle, and hand signals are allowed
   - ATA Intermediate
   - ATA Excellent
   - ATA Champion

   Verbal praise, handler enthusiasm and excitement are encouraged in all classes of competition.

   Sizes:
   - Standard: Dogs 17.1 inches and above, measured at the shoulder
   - Teacup: Dogs 17 inches and under, measured at the shoulder

   Ages:
   - Juniors-dogs 6 months to 2 years
   - Adults-dogs 2 years to 7 years
   - Seniors-dogs 7 years and over, at owners option.

4. Dogs must be registered with the ATA prior to competing in an ATA sanctioned competition. A copy of the membership card for each Handler and each dog's registration number must be furnished to the trial host each time the dog/handler team is entered into trial.

5. All ATA competitions shall be open to purebred and mixed breed dogs alike.

6. Any dog that has not previously entered an ATA competition must begin all competition at the Beginner level. A dog that runs at a level higher than they are eligible for, will not receive credit for points earned at that higher level. Points earned at a higher level prior to the completion of the lower level title, will not be added to the dogs point history.

7. Dog registration is a one-time process, and the registration number assigned is permanent.

D. Competitive Trial Approval Procedure and Requirements

1. An ATA Level II member trainer or Level III member club, association or training facility requesting to hold a sanctioned competition must make application to the ATA for an event license. Once approved, this will allow the group to designate a competitive event as "sanctioned" by ATA, and award placements, and titles.

   ATA Level II member trainer or Level III member club or facility shall comply with all the requirements set forth in these rules and regulations and other policies and guidelines as may be established by the ATA.

   This event license form is available as a pdf on our website. Forms should be filled out and emailed back 60 days prior to the date of the scheduled competition, to assure your selected date for competition.

2. The application, along with the appropriate filing fee as set forth in the event application shall be submitted to ATA in accordance with ATA policies and procedures in effect at the time. The ATA reserves the right to refuse any application for license for any reason without recourse from the requesting organization. Failure of an affiliated group to fulfill any portion of the requirements stipulated for a sanctioned trial does so at the risk of loss of sanction of the trial, match or event.

3. Only ATA affiliated groups that include a Level II or Level III member trainer will be permitted to host Treibball competitions. Any group of individuals whose goals are to promote the sport of Treibball through positive reinforcement training methods, for all breeds, may apply to ATA for approval as an affiliated group, through applying for Level III membership.

4. In addition to a completed application form, which can be obtained from our website. (Forms are currently under development.) A club, association or group seeking to become an ATA affiliated group must submit proof of insurance, a copy of the club/group's Bylaws or mission statement (in lieu of Bylaws), the name and membership number of their dedicated Treibball trainer and a list of a minimum of ten people experienced in Treibball and knowledgeable of Treibball, who are available to assist with competitions.

5. Affiliated clubs, groups or facilities must appoint a member to act as a contact person. This person shall be the liaison between ATA and the club, group or facility and is required to maintain a valid e-mail address and join the ATA Level II and III members Yahoo discussion group.

E. Hosting a Sanctioned Trial or Competition

Securing a Trial Date

1. Level II trainers and Level III member clubs or facilities will honor all trials within 300 miles of their competition site and not request dates that conflict with other ATA affiliated clubs, associations or facilities. A numbered week system will be used. The "week by number" calendar is located in the files section of the ATA Level II and III members Yahoo discussion group. Clubs should send an e-mail request for

their week number 60 days prior to the scheduled date, to secure that date and ensure that it is listed on the Calendar of Events.

2. Once a trial is confirmed and listed on the calendar, the club may then proceed to secure judges. That Level II or III member then has right of first refusal for those dates in the future.

3. Clubs may host one day, two day or three day (Fri-Sat-Sun) competitions. On a major holiday weekend, (New Years, Memorial Weekend, 4th of July, Labor Day) clubs may include Monday.

4. The number of trials a club may host each year is dependent upon the availability of dates. Contact the ATA for any scheduling conflicts unique to your area.

Trial Site

5. Hosting a trial requires a field with the following minimum dimensions:

      Standard Competition: 50 feet wide by 75 feet long

      Teacup Competition: 25 feet wide by 40 feet long

6. The trial area should be of a non-slip surface that provides a safe footing for the dogs and handlers competing.

7. Ample space should be available close by; for crating; exercise, warm-up, and for spectators to view the competition field. The ATA strongly recommends an area be set aside for warm-up, for the dogs and handlers prior to competing. If possible, the spectator's viewing area should be separate from the crating, exercise, and warm-up areas.

8. Rope/flagging tape or other adequate fencing should surround the playing field, to prevent spectators from interfering with the course area before or during the trial

9. Other amenities such as convenience for parking, camping, motels, shade, restrooms, food options, should be considered when selecting a site.

10. Host committee may allow trial runs prior to competition. Additional cost and scheduling to be determined at their discretion.

Trial/Game structure

All sanctioned trials will follow the established Game Rules of the ATA.

1. Duration of the run

Total time of each run consists of 10 minutes per dog/handler team. The dog is first placed on the start position (with 10-15 seconds to set-up), and the handler returns to his/her position at the goal line. Handler will keep his hands to his sides, until he/she signals the Timekeeper he/she is ready to start.

Official timing starts at the Timekeeper's signal. The handler then sends the dog from the start position (at 10 o'clock) midfield (to 12 o'clock), to stand behind the peak of the set-out balls.

If all eight balls are in the goal within 10 minutes time, and the dog lies down at the goal line, time is called. The Timekeepers' whistle sounds, and the run is over.

If 10 minutes are on the clock, time is called and the Timekeepers' whistle sounds. No matter how many balls are in the goal, the run is over.

2. Field of Competition Play

A trial or competition may be held indoors or outdoors, on any level playing surface.

Standard Competition: Field of 50 feet wide by 75 feet long.

Teacup Competition: Field of 25 feet wide by 40 feet long.

The perimeter of the field of competition should be clearly marked, and/or fenced, so that spectators cannot interfere with the dog and handler competing.

Beginner Classes, Divisions A & B are allowed to use Teacup Competition field dimensions, of 25 feet wide by 40 feet long, with 8 standard-sized balls.

Intermediate, Excellent and Champion classes are to compete on the Standard field dimensions of 50 feet wide by 75 feet long.

3. Ball sizes and placement

The front line of eight balls should be placed directly midfield in a triangle, with the point/peak ball placed farthest from the goal. The mid-point of the balls should be at an appropriate level to be moved by the individual competitor dog's nose or shoulder.

Standard Competition: 8 balls are used, ranging in size from 45 cm - 85 cm.

Field length of 75 feet: The front line of balls is to be placed at the 37.5 foot (midpoint) mark. Balls are to be placed with four balls in front, three balls in the center and the peak/point ball placed behind them at the farthest point from the goal line.

Oddly-shaped or weighted balls, and obstacles through which the dog must drive the balls to the goal, may be introduced in competition only at the Excellent and Champion level.

Teacup Competition: 8 balls are used. Each dog's handler is allowed to choose their preferred ball size, ranging in size from 25 cm - 45 cm, or 45 cm - 75 cm.

Field length of 40 feet: placement of the front line of balls at the 20 foot (midpoint) mark. Balls are to be placed with four balls in front, three balls in the center and the peak/point ball placed behind them, at the farthest point from the goal line.

Oddly-shaped or weighted balls, and obstacles through which the dog must drive the balls to the goal, used in Teacup Competition, must be in proportion to the competitors' size and also may be introduced only at the Excellent and Champion level.

Junior Handler members may compete in all levels of match play, in the following divisions:
   Under 10 years of age: 4-5 balls set within the playing field
   11-15 years of age: 5-6 balls set within the playing field
   14-17 years of age: 6-8 balls set within the playing field

Senior or Honors Class for handicapped handler or pets, in Standard or Teacup divisions (competitors over 65, those who have a handicap or compete with a handicapped dog) may choose to compete on a Standard or Teacup field size, with that accompanying field dimensions and ball placement. Senior or Honors competitors who have taught their dog to work on a specific side, because of impairment or mobility issues, may direct their dog from that side.

4. Goals

A regulation soccer goal can be used, a wire goal or any plastic enclosure wide and deep enough to hold eight balls (of appropriate sizes, 25 to 85 cm). Goals should be a minimum width of 5 feet deep by 12 to 14 feet long. Goals used must be deep enough to hold all eight balls, with enough room for the handler to stand in, and move within a 4 foot area, right, left and center.

The total goal area is to be defined as four feet total (48 inches) around the left, right and center of the physical goal, to allow all participants to compete equally. A goal line of vinyl tape, chalk or other demarcation should be used, to delineate the entire goal area; in front and along the left and right sides of the physical goal, so that it may be easily seen by the judges and participants.

5. Handler's Responsibility/Position

It is the handler's responsibility to see that the dog moves the ball forward with his nose, either side of his muzzle, his shoulder, chest and the backs of his front feet. The dog may use an open mouth to direct or guide the ball, but may not bite the ball or use the pads of his feet or claws to move the ball toward the handler at the goal.

The handler is allowed to position himself/herself within the 4 foot goal area, and move left, right and center within that area to direct the dog, but is not allowed to move further into the field.

The handler is allowed, *but is not required,* to use a staff of no more than 6 feet in length. The staff may be used to bring the ball into the goal once the dog has brought the ball within the 4 foot goal area but may not be used as an extension of the handler's arm, to drive the ball into the goal.

If a ball bounces out of the physical goal after being brought in by the dog, and it is still within the 4 foot goal area, the staff or a target stick may be used to bring it back into the goal. If two balls come to the goal at the same time, the staff or target stick may be used to block an undesired ball and allow a preferred ball to come in first. If the ball rolls/bounces completely outside of the goal area, it must be brought back to the goal by the dog.

In the **ATA-B, Beginner class,** Divisions A & B, the balls may be brought in any order, but the dog must work fully under the control of the handler. The handler may use a clicker in Division A, but use hand, whistle and verbal signals only, in Division B and higher. Herding whistle signals are allowed in all classes.

In the **ATA-I, Intermediate class,** it is the handler's responsibility to call out which ball the dog is to bring to him/her at the goal, (by color, shape or position) so that the Ball and Goal Line judges will see that the dog is bringing them in correctly.

In the **ATA-X Excellent class,** the Ball Judge will direct the handler (by color, shape or position) the order in which the dog will bring balls to the goal. The Ball Judge is allowed to place or reposition obstacles within the field.

In the **ATA-Ch, Champion class,** the Ball Judge will determine and direct the handler (by color, shape or position) the order in which the dog will bring balls to the goal, and decide the amount and placement of any obstacles in the field. The Ball Judge is allowed to place or reposition obstacles within the field.

6. Scoring the run

One dog and one handler compete against the clock, per run. Scoring consists of bonus or demerit points, which are subtracted or added to the dogs' score (total time allowed). Each bonus or demerit point amounts to 15 seconds off/on the clock. (Added or subtracted from the dogs' final run time.)

a. **Bonus points**—Time subtracted from total scoring:
   • 3 bonus points: With only one cue (verbal, whistle or hand signal) the dog is sent from the start position (a Down, at 10' clock to the handlers' left) to move behind the peak of the ball set, and then begins driving the ball to the handler at the goal. (45 seconds would be subtracted from total time of the run.)

- 2 bonus points: With only two cues (verbal, whistle or hand signal) the dog is sent from the start position (a Down at 10 o'clock to the handlers' left) behind the peak of the ball set, and the dog then begins driving the ball to the handler at the goal. (30 seconds would be subtracted from total time of the run.)

- 1 bonus point: Three cues (verbal or signal) are given as the dog is sent from the start position (a Down, 10' clock to the handlers' left) behind the peak of the ball set, and the dog then begins driving the ball to the handler at the goal. (15 seconds would be subtracted from total time of the run.)

b. Allowed, **but no bonus:**
- The dog drives any ball other than the one at the peak first.

- More than three cues (verbal or signal) are given to the dog before driving the first ball.

c. **Demerits**—Time added to total scoring
- 2 demerit points.
   i. The dog bites the ball or uses his claws to grasp the ball to move it forward.
   ii. The handler puts pressure on the dog by either voice or gesture. "Pressure" is here defined by the ATA as any type of aversive methods: physical punishment, threat, verbal abuse or berating. (30 seconds would be added to total time.)

- 1 demerit point.
   i. The dog starts at the incorrect side of the triangle to the handler's right of the ball set. (15 seconds would be added to total time.)
   ii. The handler enters the field in any direction: he/she moves out of the defined goal area. (15 seconds would be added to total time.)
   iii. A ball is driven out of the field. (15 seconds would be added to total time.)
   iv. The dog is barking disruptively. (15 seconds would be added to total time.) Judges should use great discretion so that those breeds that normally bark as part of their hereditary herding behavior are not penalized unfairly.
   v. The handler's staff or crook is used as an extension for driving the ball. The staff may only be used to bring the ball into the goal, once the dog has driven it within the goal area. (15 seconds would be added to total time.)

7. Disqualifications

a. The dog shows aggression to any judge on the field.

b. The dog destroys the ball by biting, even if all the balls are already in the goal.

c. The handler exerts pressure on the dog for a third time. "Pressure" is here defined by the ATA as any type of aversive methods: physical punishment, threat, verbal abuse or berating.

d. The handler punishes the dog physically.

e. The dog or handler exits the playing field during the run.

f. The dog eliminates on the field during the run.

8. Additional Rules

a. Dogs are not allowed at the immediate border of the field, and should remain out of sight while another dog is competing.

b. Treats may not be used in Adult and Junior Handler class competition. Treats may be used in Senior or Honors class competition, with the caveat that treats should not be visible on the handlers' body, and that additional physical touch and praise be used as a reward and encouragement. Senior or Honors class competition should be run last in match order, so that no treats might be left on the field to distract subsequent competitors.

c. Spectators with food are not allowed at the immediate border of the field while dogs are competing.

d. Female dogs in heat cannot participate. They may be rescheduled to compete at a later date.

e. For trials held outdoors, in case of inclement weather, the judges in conjunction with the Host Committee will decide whether the trail should be postponed or suspended.

f. Tie-breakers may be decided at the discretion of the judges in cooperation with the Host Committee.

9. Judge's Discretion

A judge has the right to inspect any dog for injury, lameness, being in season/in heat or any physical condition that might deem that dog unsafe to compete at that time. The judge may then allow or excuse that dog from competition on that date.

A judge may decide a dog should be removed from the run when he/she believes:

a. The dog has been trained by pressure. "Pressure" is here defined by the ATA as any type of aversive methods: physical punishment, threat, verbal abuse or berating.

b. The dog is under physical stress.

c. The progress of the current run is not in the dog's best interest.

10. Titling/Awards

An American Treibball Association title consists of a number of qualifying runs within the time frame designated for each division, under the aegis of two different judges. (*A qualifying run is defined as one run with any time score within the allotted time period, plus or minus any bonus or demerit points.)

Qualifying runs are based on bringing all 8 balls into the goal, within the time frame for each division.

- **ATA-Beginner**
  Division A-2 qualifying runs–time period: 10 minutes
  Division B-2 qualifying runs–time period: 10 minutes

- **ATA Intermediate**-3 qualifying runs-time period: 9 minutes

- **ATA Excellent**-4 qualifying runs-time period: 8 minutes

- **ATA Champion**-4 qualifying runs-time period: 7 minutes

- Senior or Honors competitors-2 qualifying runs–with a 2 minute allowance in each division

Awards are to be given for 1st through 4th place in each division, the following colors:

- 1st place = Blue Ribbon or Rosette

- 2nd place = Red Ribbon or Rosette

- 3rd place = Yellow Ribbon or Rosette

- 4th place = White Ribbon or Rosette

- 1-4th place, Senior/Honors = Silver Ribbon or Rosette

Toys may be given, in addition to or in lieu of, ribbons at the discretion of the Host Committee.

d. Awards are to be given for 1st through 4th place in the following class, breed and age appropriate categories, for Adults, Seniors/Honors and Junior Handlers.

- ATA-B-Beginner, Division A Division B

- ATA-I-Intermediate

- ATA-X-Excellent

- ATA-Ch.-Champion

Additional awards specific to the member club, facility or area may be given in addition to placement ribbons or toys.

F. Competition Officials/Committee

1. Competition Chairperson. The Competition Chairperson oversees the entire running of the trial before, during and after. The Competition Chairperson may also serve as Host, but may not serve as a trial judge, to avoid any conflict of interest.

The Competition Chairperson shall enforce all rules of the ATA from the time competitors are admitted on trial grounds until their departure.

The Competition Chairperson shall eliminate any competitor who is either verbally or physically abusive to any person or dog involved in the Competition. Any points this competitors dog may have earned during the

Competition shall be forfeited and no refunds will be given. The Competition Chairman shall notify the ATA in writing of any competitor eliminated from competition and the reason for the elimination.

2. Competition Secretary. The Competition Secretary shall develop the Trial schedule/ Competition Catalog for the trial and mail it and/or have it available to download for potential competitors.

The Competition Secretary is also responsible for the preparation/completion of all competition paperwork including trial results. Results of the trial should be emailed to the ATA within fifteen (15) days of the competition. The paperwork to be submitted includes:

a. The name of the affiliated host club, association or group.

b. The name and membership number of the Level II or Level III dedicated trainer of record.

c. The date and location of the trial. It is recommended that the Trial Schedule/catalog include the county in which the trial is to take place as well as GPS coordinates.

d. The names of the Judges, their town and state. Judges must be approved by ATA prior to submission of the catalog for review.

e. A description of the field surface on which the trial will be held (grass, grass/dirt, sand, matting over concrete, tree bark, etc.)

f. A listing of all entry fees for classes, age and size categories.

The Competition Secretary is also responsible to report to the ATA on the conduct and performance of Judges, Competition Management, and Competition Hosts.

3. Competition Hosts. Competition Hosts are Level II member trainer's staff, or Level III member club/group, and are the governing body for the trial. Hosts are responsible for the running of the competition including all matters other than those specifically set forth as responsibilities of the judge(s).

Competition Hosts/Host Committee is responsible for providing all equipment necessary for the execution of the trial event. Individual competitors who damage provided equipment will be expected to reimburse the Competition Hosts/Host Committee for the retail cost of any damaged equipment. (This language should be included in the Competition Hosts/Host Committee's event entry form or liability waiver.)

Competition Hosts are responsible for the reporting of, and may be involved with the resolution of, any disciplinary issues that arise.

4. ATA approved Judge(s). Each sanctioned trial/competition shall be officiated by a minimum of 2 judges from the ATA approved Judges List.

All ATA Judges are subject to the following conditions:

    a. Each Judge must be a current member of the ATA in good standing.

    b. Designation as an ATA Judge is a privilege, not a right. This privilege is granted through the Judging Committee and qualifications sought in Judges include canine experience, personal character and interest and knowledge of the sport of Treibball. Knowledge of Treibball is here defined as being a Level II or III member of the ATA in good standing, and having taught all levels of ATA Treibball for 6 months prior to the date of the trial.

    c. Judges shall not be competitors or Competition Hosts in any trial he/she is judging.

    d. Judges serve in the following capacities:

Goal Line Judge. There shall be one judge designated to stand on the sidelines, directly even/parallel with the handlers' position at the goal line. The Goal Line Judge's responsibility is to monitor action at the goal line as the balls move forward, to assure the handler keeps within the goal area.

Ball Judge. There shall be one judge designated to stand on the sidelines, directly even/parallel with the position of the point ball, behind the ball-set. The Ball Judge's responsibility is to monitor the dogs' ball control and the handler's direction to the dog.

Gate Steward. The gate steward's responsibility shall be to keep the dogs that are entered in each class in order and ready to compete.

G. After Trial Forms

    1. All required forms are to be submitted within fifteen (15) days after the date of the trial. Failure to do so may result in a fine and/or the host club/group being placed on probation, which may affect future trials. If unforeseen circumstances arise that may cause a delay, please notify the ATA immediately.

    2. Scribe Sheets/marked catalog - kept by club. Scribe sheets and copies of marked catalogs are to be kept by the club/group for a period of six months.

Marked Catalog—The catalog pages must be clearly identified by listing the Level II Trainer or Level III Club/Group, Name, Competition Date, Judge(s), Class, Level, Division, and Category on each page. The dog's time, time faults, and total faults must be clearly indicated. The catalog must also include each dog's ATA Registration number, and Owner's last name for each entry for each class.

Clubs/Association groups are not required to submit copies of the fully marked Catalog. We ask that the completed Catalog be kept on file by the club/group for a minimum of 1 year.

H. Record keeping

1. Competitors List—send to the ATA. A complete list of competitors is due when submitting results of a trial or competition. This list is to include the names and addresses of the registered owners of the dogs entered in the competition. E-mail addresses are encouraged, but not required.

2. Recording Fees—send to the ATA. The recording fees are due when submitting results. Fees shall be submitted for ALL runs listed in the catalog, including runs in which a dog was entered but scratched or did not compete.

3. Trial Report Form—send to the ATA. This form is to be filled out by the Competition Chairperson or Secretary and mailed to ATA with the competitor's list and recording fees.

4. There is a $25.00 per day fee for late submissions. If unable to comply with the 15 day requirement, contact us to request an extension.

5. When accepting entries and inputting them into your catalog, it is imperative that the dog's registration number and the competitors' member number is valid and correct.

6. Day of Trial entries may be allowed only if the classes competing on that date are not full. The Host Club may assign a temporary membership and registration number to Day of Trial entrants. When the paperwork is submitted to and logged by the ATA, this number will be replaced by official dog and member numbers, their titles or points will be registered and the entrant will be informed of the correct registration numbers to be used henceforth.

7. The ATA maintains a list of dog registration numbers linked from our website at http://www.americantribballassociation.org . The file lists the dog's registration number, call name, registered name, and owner's first and last name. An 'NP' in place of the dog's registered name indicates that ATA has not received the registration fee. New registration numbers will be added to this list monthly. Any corrections, changes, transfers in ownership are updated periodically. When verifying a registration number, the number and the dog's call name should match. If there is a question, please contact the ATA. Level II and III member trainers and clubs may submit questions or share information via americantreibballassociation@yahoogroups.com

I. Competitor Communications:

Notice should be provided to all competitors with the following information provided:

1. A full explanation of official ATA game rules and up to date trial information.

2. ATA competitions provide a safe and fun environment for both exhibitors and their dogs.

3. Dogs exhibiting aggressive/reactive behavior will not be tolerated and will be excused from the trial.

4. The ATA affiliated clubs' Trial/Host Committee retains the right to refuse any entry. Anyone not currently in good standing with ATA will not be allowed to enter the trial.

5. Competitors, through submission of entry, acknowledge that they are knowledgeable of ATA rules and regulations, and agree to abide by all rules in elect at the time of this competition.

6. Entry fees will not be refunded if the competition cannot open or be completed by reasons of riots, civil disturbances, fire, acts of nature, public emergency, and an act of a public enemy, or any other cause beyond the control of the ATA affiliated clubs' Host/organizing committee.

7. Checks for entry fees not honored by the bank do not constitute a valid entry. Any points earned in competition by an invalid entry will be forfeited. There will be a service charge for any returned checks.

8. All dogs must be registered with a valid registration number before trial entries will be accepted.

9. Members and non-members may download a free copy of the current Sanctioned Trial and Competition Rules from our website, www.americantreibballassociation.org, under the Merchandise tab. Level II and III members may also download a free copy of the current Sanctioned Trial and Competition Rules from the files section of the americantreibballassociation@yahoogroups.com

10. Day of Trial entries may be allowed only if the classes competing on that date are not full. The Host Club may assign a temporary membership and registration number to Day of Trial entrants. When the paperwork is submitted to and logged by the ATA, this number will be replaced by official dog and member numbers, their titles or points will be registered and the entrant will be informed of the correct registration numbers to be used henceforth.

11. The ATA maintains a list of dog registration numbers linked from our website at http://www.americantribballassociation.org. The file lists the dog's registration number, call name, registered name, and owner's first and last name. An 'NP' in place of the dog's registered name indicates that ATA has not received the registration fee. New registration numbers will be added to this list monthly. Any corrections, changes, transfers in ownership are updated periodically. When verifying a registration number, the number and the dog's call name should match. If there is a question, please contact the ATA. Level II and III member trainers and clubs may submit questions or share information via americantreibballassociation@yahoogroups.com .

© 2013, Copyright American Treibball Association, a 501(c)3 non-profit corporation

Glossary of Terms

Away to Me: Verbal cue used to send your dog counter-clockwise, to your left.

Back: Cue used to cue dog to move backward, in a straight line, in progressive steps.

Back-chaining: Technique that marks and rewards each individual step, moving from the last step back to the first, before connecting all the steps together into a completed behavior.

Clicker: Small plastic and metal sound maker, used to mark desired behavior as it happens. Available at most retail dog suppliers in different configurations, with differing levels of sound.

Come Bye: Short for "Come by the clock." Verbal cue used to send your dog clockwise, to your right.

Criteria: A certain standard or rule, by which a particular judgment can be made. For example, if your dog is consistently putting his nose on the ball at the midpoint, you would raise your criteria (your standard) to reward only those stronger pushes on the ball at the midpoint, that move the ball forward.

Cue: An action or sound given to your dog that signals the beginning of another action, such as Sit or Come.

Directional cues: Away to Me, Back, Come Bye, Out, and Walk-on: verbal cues that tell your dog which way to go, or how to move to gather the selected ball.

Down: Verbal cue used to have your dog lie with all four feet and his belly in contact with the ground.

Drive: Cue used to have the dog move the ball forward, using his nose or shoulder, to the handler at the goal. You may also use "Push" if that comes more naturally to you.

Fade: The gradual diminishing of a cue or reward being given, once the desired behavior has become reliable.

Fluency: The ability of a movement or action capable of being done with ease; smoothness of execution.

Ground target: A flat, visual marker, placed on the ground to provide a station or a contact point for your dog.

Jackpot: Extra "high-value" assortment of treats/rewards, usually consisting of 4 or 5 different tastes and textures, used to reward the dog for the most difficult or most exceptional execution of a cue.

Line-up: Verbal cue used to position your dog squarely behind the ball, with all four legs in line with each other and perpendicular to you, before driving the ball to the goal.

Mark: Any sound or tone used to immediately designate the just-performed behavior as being correct, such as the sound of the clicker, or the verbal word like "Yes!"

Primary: The actual reward your dog is willing to work for, such as treat, a Frisbee

Reinforcer: toss, a tummy rub. Whatever motivates your dog to work can be used as a reinforcer for that work.

(Go) Out: Cue used to move your dog farther down the field, before adding a directional cue.

Release word: A short word or phrase that's used to tell your dog he has completed the task you asked for. In this curriculum we use **That'll do!** to release the dog once all the balls are in the goal, or time is called.

Shaping: Technique used to "get" a behavior, mark and reward each individual step (or correct attempt) in small increments, with the goal of linking those steps into a completed behavior.

Secondary: Something that is paired with the primary reinforcer, to communicate

Reinforcer: to the dog that his reward, the primary reinforcer, is coming. This is also sometimes referred to as a "bridge", and the clicker or a verbal marker like "Yes!' serves this purpose.

Staff: A 6 foot wooden stick/pole used to help guide balls into the goal after your dog brings them to the goal line. Your 3-4 foot target stick may also be used for this.

Stand: Verbal cue used to hold your dog in an upright position behind the balls, with his body weight balanced equally, on all four feet.

Standard size: Dogs measuring 17.1 inches or more at the shoulder.

Start position: The Start position is defined as being 21 feet from the zero-foot mark and 7 feet inside the left side of the field, for Toy breeds/Teacup competition, and 33 feet from the zero-foot mark and 9 feet inside the left side of the field, for Standard size dogs.

Targeting: Focusing technique used in cueing your dog to touch your hand, or an object with his nose or paw.

Target stick: A high visibility tool, 3 to four feet in length, used as an extension of your arm to focus your dog's attention, and give him direction at distance from you.

That'll do: Herding cue used to release your dog from his duties, after all the "sheep" (or balls) are in the pen.

Touch: Cue used to signal your dog to make contact with your hand, a target stick or the ball, using only his nose or shoulder.

Toy/Teacup size: Those dogs measuring 17 inches or less at the shoulder.

Walk-on: Herding cue used to encourage your dog to move up slowly, step-by-step, from behind without over-shooting the position of the "sheep" (or balls.)

Watch me: Verbal cue and hand used to signal your dog to make direct eye contact with you.

Resources

Treibball videos, training tips and information: Visit www.americantreibballassociation.org for new training tips and videos, upcoming events and an ATA member/trainer locator, to find a Certified American Treibball trainer and a class near you. You'll also find us on Facebook at www.facebook.com/americantreibball and see more videos at www.youtube.com/user/AmericanTreibball

Exercise balls: Inexpensive standard vinyl and anti-burst vinyl balls are available in the exercise equipment section at most sporting goods stores and at national, big box retailers across the U.S. (Sports Authority, Big 5 Sports, Target, Wal-Mart, Kmart, etc.). Ball sizes 25 cm to 45 cm are recommended for Toy breed/Small sized dogs, measuring 17 inches or less at the shoulder. Sizes 45 cm to 75 cm are recommended for those dogs measuring 17.1 and higher at the shoulder.

Specialty balls: Specialty egg and "peanut" shaped balls for advanced play, are available from FitPaws Canine Conditioning Equipment, www.balldynamics.com/fitpaw 800-752-2255, Canine Spirit Balls (balls that come with a nylon tough cover, for play on rough terrains) are available from www.Canine-Spirit-Ball.com, and heavier weight, vinyl balls are available from www.TeamBumper.com.

Clickers: Individual clickers are available at most independently owned pet supply shops and at major pet retailers, such as Petco and PETsMART. Imprintable box clickers are available from Wayne Hightower, 800-246-6336, and The Clicker Company, www.clickercompany.com 480-706-1884. Softer tone iclick clickers are available from Arcata Pet Supplies, www.arcata.com 800-822-9085, and the Clicker Company, www.clicker-company.com 480-706-1884.

Herding whistles: Available online from Border Collies in Action, www.bordercollies.com, 800-833-0322

Leashes/long lines: J & J Dog Supplies www.jjdog.com 1-309-344-2950, PetEdge, www.PetEdge.com 1-800-738-3343, and at major pet retailers, such as Petco and PETsMART.

Target stick supplies: 3 foot and 4 foot wooden dowels are available at craft and hardware stores such as Home Depot, Lowe's, Hobby Lobby and Michael's Art supplies. 4 foot sticks should be used with teacup-sized dogs, 17 inches and under; and shorter, 3 foot sticks should be used with standard-sized dogs, 17 inches and up, measured at the shoulder. Practice foam golf balls are available in sporting goods departments.

Toy rewards: Kong Company, www.KONGcompany.com, and Katie's Bumpers, www.katiesbumpers.com, make great rewards.

ABOUT THE AUTHOR

Dianna Stearns is a Certified Professional Dog Trainer-Knowledge Assessed, a Certified Dog Behavior Consultant, and the owner of Waggin's West Dog Training and Behavior Consulting, LLC, in Northglenn, Colorado. As a life-long dog lover, Dianna established Waggin's West Dog Training and Behavior Consulting in 2005 to provide dog owners a gentle, effective alternative to the punishment-based methods that some national franchise operations and TV trainers espouse.

Dianna serves as a trainer and behavior consultant for four regional breed rescue organizations, and two human-centered non-profits, to provide public access training for assistance dogs. Dianna is a professional member of the Association of Pet Dog Trainers, the International Association of Animal Behavior Consultants, the Pet Professionals Guild for force-free training, and is an American Kennel Club Canine Good Citizen evaluator.

As the author of numerous magazine articles on behavior issues and positive reinforcement training, she continues to stay informed of current behavioral research, in order to offer clients the most up-to-date training methods and techniques. Dianna is a co-founder and currently serves as President of the American Treibball Association.

INDEX

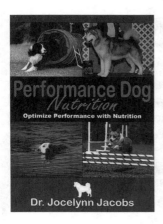

Performance Dog Nutrition
Optimize Performance with Nutrition
Dr. Jocelynn Jacobs

The first and only nutrition book written for performance dogs!
Veterinarian, musher, obedience competitor and breeder, Dr. Jocelynn Jacobs, saw the need for sound, scientific nutritional information in her busy veterinary practice and in the world of canine sports. She realized that much of what is passed around the dog world as facts about ingredients and canine nutrition are less than scientific and sometimes downright dangerous for the dog. Dr. Jacobs created this book to help competitors in a wide range of dog sports improve performance and get great results. The information is also useful for the dog owner who wants to learn more about canine nutrition without the marketing hype.

2006 DWAA Maxwell Award Winner—Best Care and Health Book Category

The Healthy Way to Stretch Your Dog
A Physical Therapy Approach
Sasha Foster and Ashley Foster

Stretch your dog to a longer and healthier life
Research on human athletes is changing what we know about stretching. For example, it is now recognized that aggressive stretching should only take place after muscles are warmed up and shortened from exertion. Authors Sasha and Ashley Foster have applied this latest research to dogs—many of whom compete in vigorous canine sporting events—so that you can learn how to safely and effectively stretch your dog to prevent injuries, maintain joint integrity, and improve you dog's fitness whether he is an elite canine athlete or a lap dog.

Over 300 photos and diagrams demonstrate how to safely and effectively stretch each major muscle group. Teaches correct hand placement for joint stabilization and how to maintain good form. Stretching routines are presented for both large and small dogs, older dogs, and those that are involved in a variety of dog sports.

2009 DWAA Maxwell Award Winner—Best Care and Health Book Category

Dogwise.com your source for quality books, ebooks, DVDs, training tools and treats.

We've been selling to the dog fancier for more than 25 years and we carefully screen our products for quality information, safety, durability and FUN! You'll find something for every level of dog enthusiast on our website www.dogwise.com or drop by our store in Wenatchee, Washington.

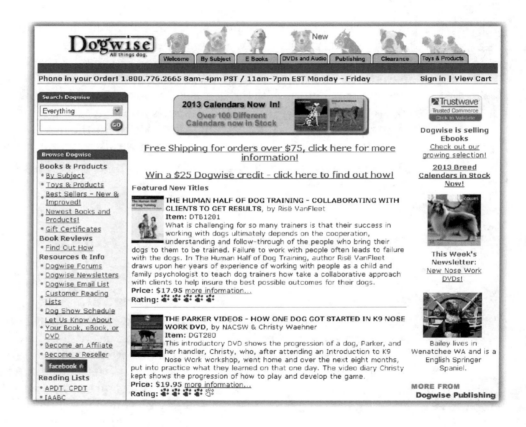